CW01659265

SONGS OF FELLOWSHIP

Large Print Words Edition

Volume 2

Songs of Fellowship

LARGE PRINT WORDS EDITION
Volume 2

KINGSWAY MUSIC
EASTBOURNE

First published 1999.

ISBN 0 85476 821 1

Designed and produced by Bookprint Creative Services
P.O. Box 827, BN21 3YJ, England for
KINGSWAY COMMUNICATIONS LTD
Lottbridge Drove, Eastbourne, East Sussex, BN23 6NT, UK.
Printed in Great Britain.

641

Bob Baker.

ABRAHAM'S SON, Chosen One,
Zion's cornerstone;
Passover Lamb, Son of Man,
Seated upon Your throne.

Hail to the King,
Hail to the King,
Hail to the King of kings.
(Repeat)

O promised Seed, beneath Your feet
Sin and death shall fall.
Now through us tread the serpent's head
Till You are all in all.

The world's yet to see Your glory,
But You'll be revealed in power,
And You will reign with the Bride ordained
For Your consummating hour.

642

Paul Oakley.

ALL AROUND THE WORLD *there's a new day dawning,*
There's a sound coming round,
There's a new song rising up,
Ah, it's a new day!
Everywhere you go you can hear this story,
There's a power coming down,
There's a glimpse of glory now,
Ah, it's a new day!

There's a sound of praise,
There's a sound of war;
Lift the banner high, let the Lion roar.
Can you hear the sound in the tops of the trees?
Heaven's armies come! Crush the enemy!

Let the lame run, let the blind see!
Let Your power come, set the captives free!
Let the lost return to the Lover of our souls,
Let the prodigal find the way back home.

Lift your hands before the King,
The sovereign Ruler of the earth;
Let the nations come to Him,
Let the cry of hearts be heard:

Revive us! Revive us! Revive us again!
(Repeat)

643

Randy Wright.

ALL CONSUMING FIRE,
You're my heart's desire,
And I love You dearly, dearly Lord.
You're my meditation,
And my consolation,
And I love You dearly, dearly Lord.

Glory to the Lamb,
I exalt the great I AM;
Reigning on Your glorious throne,
You are my eternal home.

644

Mike Blow.

ALL CREATION BOWS at the name of Jesus,
Every star is in His hands.
Yet the glorious mystery of ages,
He delights in fragile man.

There is mercy in the name of Jesus,
Mercy to forgive our sin.
The mighty King of heaven became the humble servant,
To bring His children back to Him.
And this is why I will sing:

Hallelujah, Christ is risen,
Hallelujah, we are saved.
He has purchased our salvation,
Hallelujah, praise His name.

There is shelter in the name of Jesus,
He accepts the refugee;
And His mighty strength will never fail us,
His arm is always close to me.
And all my life I will sing:

645

St Francis of Assisi.
Tr. William Henry Draper.

ALL CREATURES OF OUR GOD AND KING,
Lift up your voice and with us sing:
Hallelujah, hallelujah!
Thou burning sun with golden beam,
Thou silver moon with softer gleam:

O praise Him, O praise Him,
Hallelujah, hallelujah, hallelujah!

Thou rushing wind that art so strong,
Ye clouds that sail in heaven along,
O praise Him, hallelujah!
Thou rising morn, in praise rejoice,
Ye lights of evening, find a voice:

Thou flowing water, pure and clear,
Make music for thy Lord to hear,
Hallelujah, hallelujah!
Thou fire so masterful and bright,
That givest man both warmth and light:

And all ye men of tender heart,
Forgiving others, take your part,
O sing ye, hallelujah!
Ye who long pain and sorrow bear,
Praise God and on Him cast your care:

Let all things their Creator bless,
And worship Him in humbleness,
O praise Him, hallelujah!
Praise, praise the Father, praise the Son,
And praise the Spirit, Three-in-One:

646

Graham Kendrick

ALL I ONCE HELD DEAR, built my life upon,
All this world reveres, and wars to own,
All I once thought gain I have counted loss;
Spent and worthless now, compared to this.

Knowing You, Jesus,
Knowing You, there is no greater thing.
You're my all, You're the best,
You're my joy, my righteousness,
And I love You, Lord.

Now my heart's desire is to know You more,
To be found in You and known as Yours.
To possess by faith what I could not earn,
All-surpassing gift of righteousness.

Oh, to know the power of Your risen life,
And to know You in Your sufferings.
To become like You in Your death, my Lord,
So with You to live and never die.

647

James Wright.

ALL THAT I AM *I lay before You;*
All I possess, Lord, I confess
Is nothing without You.
Saviour and King, I now enthrone You;
Take my life, my living sacrifice to You.

Lord, be the strength within my weakness;
Be the supply in every need,
That I may prove Your promises to me,
Faithful and true in word and deed.

Into Your hands I place the future;
The past is nailed to Calvary,
That I may live in resurrection power,
No longer I but Christ in me.

648

David Fellingham.

ALL THE ENDS OF THE EARTH will remember,
And turn to the Lord of glory;
All the families of the nations will bow down to the Lord,
As His righteous acts of power are displayed.

And we will awaken the nations,
To bring their worship to Jesus.
And righteousness and praise shall spring forth
In all the earth.
And we will awaken the nations,
To bring their worship to Jesus,
And the kingdom shall be revealed in power,
With signs, wonders and miracles,
And righteousness and praise shall spring forth
In all the earth.

Who will not fear the Lord of glory,
Or bring honour to His holy name?
For God has spoken with integrity and truth,
A word which cannot be revoked.

649

Jan Harrington.

ALL THE RICHES OF HIS GRACE,
All the fulness of His blessings,
All the sweetness of His love
He gives to you,
He gives to me.

Oh, the blood of Jesus,
Oh, the blood of Jesus,
Oh, the blood of Jesus,
It washes white as snow.

Oh, the word of Jesus,
Oh, the word of Jesus,
Oh, the word of Jesus,
It cleanses white as snow.

Oh, the love of Jesus,
Oh, the love of Jesus,
Oh, the love of Jesus,
It makes His Body whole.

650 John Gibson.

(Leader) **ALL YOU PEOPLE,**
(All) *Sing unto the Lord.*
(Leader) *All you nations,*
(All) *Sing unto the Lord.*
Come with dancing,
Come and raise Your voice to the King,
Come and sing unto the Lord.

From the sun's rising
To the sun's setting,
In every place, every land,
He will be glorified;
Offerings of worship from every nation,
Let every tribe, every tongue,
Join in one song of praise.

(Leader) People of Africa,...
(All) Sing unto the Lord. *(After each line)*
Europe and Asia,...
All of Australasia,...
And all across America,...
The rich and poor will ...
The weak and strong can ...
Every generation, ...
Every tribe and nation, ...

651 Nathan Fellingham & Adrian Watts.

ALMIGHTY GOD, I have heard of Your fame;
I stand in awe of Your wondrous deeds.
The heavens declare Your glorious name;
I worship You above all my needs.

The skies display the work of Your hands,
I will praise You for the rest of my days.
Who can You ask to approve Your plans?
For You are sovereign in all of Your ways.

I will only worship You,
There is nothing I want more
Than to be with You,
More and more I love You, Lord.
The only One I bow before,
I worship You with all that You've put in me;
This is what You made me for.

652

Darlene Zschech.

ALMIGHTY GOD, MY REDEEMER,
My hiding place, my safe refuge;
No other name like Jesus,
No power can stand against You.

My feet are planted on this rock,
And I will not be shaken;
My hope it comes from You alone,
My Lord and my salvation.

Your praise is always on my lips,
Your word is living in my heart,
And I will praise You with a new song:
My soul will bless You, Lord.
You fill my life with greater joy;
Yes, I delight myself in You,
And I will praise You with a new song:
My soul will bless You, Lord.

When I am weak, You make me strong;
When I'm poor, I know I'm rich,
For in the power of Your name
All things are possible. (x4)

653

Carol Owen.

AMONG THE GODS there is none like You,
O Lord, O Lord.
There are no deeds to compare with Yours, O Lord.
All the nations You have made will come;
They'll worship before You, O Lord,
O Lord.

For You are great and do marvellous deeds.
Yes, You are great and do marvellous deeds.
You alone are God, You alone are God.

You are so good and forgiving,
O Lord, O Lord.
You're rich in love to all who call to You.
All the nations You have made will come;
They'll glorify Your name, O Lord,
O Lord.

Teach me Your ways, O Lord,
And I'll walk in Your truth.
Give me an undivided heart,
That I may fear Your name.

654

Mark Altrogge.

AND FROM YOUR FULNESS *we have all received*
Grace upon grace,
Kindness on kindness.
And from Your fulness we have all received
Grace upon grace,
Like wave upon wave
From the ocean of Your love.

Lord, You stand willing
And ready to bless,
You bid us bring You
Great requests;
Though many are saying
'Who will show us good?'
Day after day we see Your mercies.

Lord, You're the Author
Of every good gift;
You give us all
We need to live.
Lord, You became poor
To make us rich,
You crown our lives with Your compassion.

655

Graham Kendrick.

AND HE SHALL REIGN *forever,*
His throne and crown shall ever endure.
And He shall reign forever,
And we shall reign with Him.

What a vision filled my eyes,
One like a Son of man,
Coming with the clouds of heaven
He approached an awesome throne.

He was given sovereign power,
Glory and authority.
Every nation, tribe and tongue
Worshipped Him on bended knee.

On the throne forever,
See the Lamb who once was slain.
Wounds of sacrificial love
Forever shall remain.

656 Donn Thomas.

ANOINTING, FALL ON ME,
Anointing, fall on me;
Let the power of the Holy Ghost
Fall on me,
Anointing, fall on me.

Touch my hands, my mouth and my heart;
Fill my life, Lord, every part.
Let the power of the Holy Ghost
Fall on me,
Anointing, fall on me.

657 Noel & Tricia Richards.

ARE WE THE PEOPLE
Who will see God's kingdom come,
When He is known in every nation?
One thing is certain,
We are closer than before;
Keep moving on, last generation.

These are the days for harvest,
To gather in the lost;
Let those who live in darkness
Hear the message of the cross.

We'll go where God is sending,
We'll do what He commands;
These years that He has waited
Could be coming to an end.

658 Richard Lewis.

AS THE DEER PANTS for the water,
So my soul, it thirsts for You,
For You, O God,
For You, O God.
(Repeat)

When can I come before You
And see Your face?
My heart and my flesh cry out
For the living God,
For the living God.

Deep calls to deep
At the thunder of Your waterfalls.
Your heart of love is calling out to me.
By this I know that I am Yours
And You are mine.
Your waves of love are breaking over me.
Your waves of love are breaking over me.
Your waves of love are breaking over me.

659 Timothy Dudley-Smith.

AS WATER TO THE THIRSTY,
As beauty to the eyes,
As strength that follows weakness,
As truth instead of lies;
As songtime and springtime
And summertime to be,
So is my Lord,
My living Lord,
So is my Lord to me.

Like calm in place of clamour,
Like peace that follows pain,
Like meeting after parting,
Like sunshine after rain;
Like moonlight and starlight
And sunlight on the sea,
So is my Lord,
My living Lord,
So is my Lord to me.

As sleep that follows fever,
As gold instead of grey,
As freedom after bondage,
As sunrise to the day;
As home to the traveller
And all he longs to see,
So is my Lord,
My living Lord,
So is my Lord to me.

660

David Baroni.

AS WE BEHOLD YOU, as we behold You,
We are changing into Your image.
As we behold You, as we behold You,
We are changing from glory to glory.

As we behold You in all of Your glory,
Lord, by Your Spirit we are changing
Into Your image from glory to glory,
As we behold You, living God.

661

Lex Loizides.

AS WE SEE THE WORLD in tatters,
As we watch their dreams break down,
We can hear their quiet anguish:
'Come and help us!'
Brought to life by God's own Spirit,
Joined together in His Son,
Now the church with strength arises
Like an army.

Every place, every place
Where our feet shall tread,
Every tribe, every race
God has given us.

In the midst of boastful darkness
Shines a Light that cannot fail,
And the blind behold His glory,
Jesus! Jesus!
Not content with restoration
Of the remnant in the land,
He has filled us with His power
For the nations.

662

Derek Bond.

AT THE FOOT OF THE CROSS,
I can hardly take it in,
That the King of all creation
Was dying for my sin.
And the pain and agony,
And the thorns that pierced Your head,
And the hardness of my sinful heart
That left You there for dead.

And O what mercy I have found
At the cross of Calvary;
I will never know Your loneliness,
All on account of me.
And I will bow my knee before Your throne,
'cause Your love has set me free;
And I will give my life to You, dear Lord,
And praise Your majesty,
And praise Your majesty,
And praise Your majesty.

663

Gill Broomhall.

BABY JESUS IN THE MANGER,
To the world He's still a stranger.
Wise men bring their gifts
Of gold and myrrh,
Baby Jesus in the manger.

Noel, Noel, Noel,
Hail the Immanuel.

Gentle Jesus, meek and lowly,
Full of love so pure and holy.
He will teach and pray,
Show mankind the way,
Gentle Jesus, meek and lowly.

Loving Jesus, mocked and beaten,
He the sin of man has taken.
He has paid the price,
He has given His life,
Loving Jesus, mocked and beaten.

Mighty Jesus, He is risen,
He has broken out of prison.
He has conquered sin,
Brought new life to men,
Mighty Jesus, He is risen.

664

Graham Kendrick.

BEAUTY FOR BROKENNESS,
Hope for despair,
Lord, in Your suffering world
This is our prayer:
Bread for the children,
Justice, joy, peace;
Sunrise to sunset,
Your kingdom increase!

Shelter for fragile lives,
Cures for their ills,
Work for the craftsman,
Trade for their skills;
Land for the dispossessed,
Rights for the weak,
Voices to plead the cause
Of those who can't speak.

God of the poor,
Friend of the weak,
Give us compassion we pray:
Melt our cold hearts,
Let tears fall like rain;
Come, change our love
From a spark to a flame.

Refuge from cruel wars,
Havens from fear,
Cities for sanctuary,
Freedoms to share;

Peace to the killing-fields,
Scorched earth to green,
Christ for the bitterness,
His cross for the pain.

Rest for the ravaged earth,
Oceans and streams
Plundered and poisoned—
Our future, our dreams.
Lord, end our madness,
Carelessness, greed;
Make us content with
The things that we need.

Lighten our darkness,
Breathe on this flame
Until Your justice
Burns brightly again;
Until the nations
Learn of Your ways,
Seek Your salvation
And bring You their praise.

665

Dave Bilbrough.

BE FREE *in the love of God,*
Let His Spirit flow within you.
Be free in the love of God,
Let it fill your soul.
Be free in the love of God,
Celebrate His name with dancing.
Be free in the love of God,
He has made us whole.

For His purpose He has called us,
In His hands He will uphold us.
He will keep us and sustain us
In the Father's love.

God is gracious, He will lead us
Through His power at work within us.
Spirit, guide us, and unite us
In the Father's love.

666

Billy Funk.

BE GLORIFIED, be glorified.
Be glorified, be glorified.
Be glorified in the heavens,
Be glorified in the earth;
Be glorified in the temple,
Jesus, Jesus,
Be Thou glorified.
Jesus, Jesus,
Be Thou glorified.

Worship the Lord, worship the Lord.
Worship the Lord, worship the Lord.
Worship the Lord in the heavens,
Worship the Lord in the earth;
Worship the Lord in the temple,
Jesus, Jesus,
Be Thou glorified.
Jesus, Jesus,
Be Thou glorified.

667

Gerald Coates & Noel Richards.

BEHOLD THE LORD upon His throne;
His face is shining like the sun.
With eyes blazing fire, and feet glowing bronze,
His voice like mighty water roars.
Holy, holy, Lord God Almighty.
Holy, holy, we stand in awe of You.

The First, the Last, the living One
Laid down His life for all the world;
Behold He now lives forever more,
And holds the keys of death and hell.
Holy, holy, Lord God Almighty;
Holy, holy, we bow before Your throne.

So let our praises ever ring
To Jesus Christ, our glorious King.
All heaven and earth resound as we cry:
'Worthy is the Son of God!'
Holy, holy, Lord God Almighty;
Holy, holy, we fall down at Your feet.

668 Charles Wesley.

BEHOLD THE SERVANT OF THE LORD:
I wait Thy guiding eye to feel,
To hear and keep Thy every word,
To prove and do Thy perfect will;
Joyful from my own works to cease,
Glad to fulfil all righteousness.

Me if Thy grace vouchsafe to use,
Meanest of all Thy creatures, me.
The deed, the time, the manner choose:
Let all my fruit be found of Thee.
Let all my works in Thee be wrought,
By Thee to full perfection brought.

My every weak though good design
O'errule or change, as seems Thee meet:
Jesus, let all my work be Thine –
Thy work, O Lord, is all complete,
And pleasing in Thy Father's sight;
Thou only hast done all things right.

Here then to Thee Thine own I leave;
Mould as Thou wilt Thy passive clay;
But let me all Thy stamp receive,
But let me all Thy words obey,
Serve with a single heart and eye,
And in Thy glory live and die.

669

James Montgomery.

BE KNOWN TO US IN BREAKING BREAD,
But do not then depart;
Saviour, abide with us, and spread
Thy table in our heart.

There sup with us in love divine;
Thy body and Thy blood,
That living bread, that heavenly wine,
Be our immortal food.

We would not live by bread alone,
But by Thy word of grace,
In strength of which we travel on
To our abiding place.

670

Jim Bailey.

BELLS THEY ARE RINGING,
Children are singing,
And we are exalting the Name over all.
Flags they are dancing,
The church is advancing,
As we are romancing the Name over all.

Jesus' kingdom can't be shaken,
Jesus' promise can't be broken,
Jesus, Lord of all creation,
Name over all.

Jesus, Truth of liberation,
Jesus, Light of our salvation,
Jesus, only way to heaven,
The Name over all.

671

Lex Loizides.

BE STILL AND KNOW that I am God:
I will be glorified and praised in all the earth.
For My great name I will be found,
And I can never be resisted,
Never be undone;
I'm never lacking power
To glorify My Son.
The gates of hell are falling
And the church is coming forth,
My name will be exalted in the earth.

Be still and know that I am God;
I have poured out My Holy Spirit like a flood.
The land that cries for holy rain
Shall be inheriting her promises
And dancing like a child;
A holy monsoon deluge
Shall bless the barren heights,
And those who sat in silence
Shall speak up and shall be heard:
My name will be exalted in the earth.

Be still and know that I am God;
My Son has asked me for
The nations of the world.
His sprinkled blood has made a way
For all the multitudes of India and Africa to come;
The Middle East will find its peace

Through Jesus Christ My Son.
From London down to Cape Town,
From L.A. to Beijing,
My Son shall reign the undisputed King!

672

John L. Bell & Graham Maule.

BE STILL AND KNOW THAT I AM GOD.
Be still and know that I am God.

673

Clinton Utterbach.

BLESSÈD BE THE NAME OF THE LORD,
Blessed be the name of the Lord,
Blessed be the name of the Lord Most High!
(Repeat)

The Name of the Lord is a strong tower,
The righteous run into it,
And they are saved.
(Repeat)

Glory to the name of the Lord...

Holy is the name of the Lord...

674

Joey Holder.

BLESSÈD JESUS, come to me,
Soothe my soul with songs of peace.
As I look to You alone,
Fill me with Your love.

Glorious, marvellous
Grace that rescued me;
Holy, worthy
Is the Lamb who died for me.

Mountains high and valleys low,
You will never let me go;
By Your fountain let me drink,
Fill my thirsty soul.

675

Gary Sadler & Jamie Harvill.

BLESSING AND HONOUR, glory and power
Be unto the Ancient of Days;
From every nation, all of creation
Bow before the Ancient of Days.

Every tongue in heaven and earth
Shall declare Your glory,
Every knee shall bow at Your throne
In worship;
You will be exalted, O God,
And Your kingdom shall not pass away,
O Ancient of Days.

Your kingdom shall reign over all the earth:
Sing unto the Ancient of Days.
For none shall compare to Your matchless worth:
Sing unto the Ancient of Days.

676

Jacques Berthier/Taizé.

BLESS THE LORD, MY SOUL,
And bless God's holy name.
Bless the Lord, my soul,
Who leads me into life.

It is God who forgives all your guilt,
Who heals every one of your ills,
Who redeems your life from the grave,
Who crowns you with love and compassion.

The Lord is compassion and love,
The Lord is patient and rich in mercy.
God does not treat us according to our sins,
Nor repay us according to our faults.

As a father has compassion on his children,
The Lord has mercy on those who revere Him;
For God knows of what we are made,
And remembers that we are dust.

677

Tina Pownall.

BREATHE ON ME, Spirit of Jesus.
Breathe on me, Holy Spirit of God.

Fill me again, Spirit of Jesus.
Fill me again, Holy Spirit of God.

Change my heart, Spirit of Jesus.
Change my heart, Holy Spirit of God.

Bring peace to the world, Spirit of Jesus.
Bring peace to the world, Holy Spirit of God.

678

Edwin Hatch, adpt. David Fellingham.

BREATHE ON ME, BREATH OF GOD,
And fill my life anew;
That I may love as You love,
And do the works that You do.
Holy Spirit, breathe on me.

Breathe on me, breath of God,
Until my heart is pure;
Until my will is one with Yours
Let holiness and love endure.
Holy Spirit, breathe on me.

And let every part of me
Glow with fire divine;
With passion in my life,
Jesus, let Your glory shine.
(Repeat)

679 Kent & Carla Henry.

BURN IT DEEP within my soul,
New strength and fire, O Lord.
Burn it deep within my soul,
New zeal and fire, O Lord.
Burn it deep within my soul,
New strength and fire,
It makes me whole.
Burn it deep,
Deep within my soul.

And You came
With the Holy Spirit's desire.
You came
With a zeal for Your Father's house.
Consume me, Lord,
With Your purifying fire,
And strengthen me
By Your mighty hand.

680

David Fellingham.

BY YOUR BLOOD I can enter the holiest place,
To the throne of my Father and King.
There I find Your acceptance, mercy and grace,
And my life is renewed again.

Far away from the stress and the turmoil of life,
I now come to seek Your face.
In the house of the Lord where Your presence is found,
I now come to worship You.

I see the King upon the throne,
Jesus, full of majesty.
I will fall down at Your feet,
I will worship You alone.

In the light of Your presence I find deepest joy,
There is no other place I would be.
To behold Your beauty is all my desire,
You're the one my heart longs for,
You're the one my heart longs for.

681

Noel & Tricia Richards.

CALLED TO A BATTLE, heavenly war;
Though we may struggle, victory is sure.
Death will not triumph, though we may die;
Jesus has promised our eternal life.

By the blood of the Lamb we shall overcome,
See the accuser thrown down.
By the word of the Lord we shall overcome,
Raise a victory cry,
Like thunder in the skies,
Thunder in the skies.

Standing together, moving as one;
We are God's army, called to overcome.
We are commissioned, Jesus says go;
In every nation, let His love be known.

682

Matt Redman.

CAN A NATION BE CHANGED?
Can a nation be saved?
Can a nation be turned back to You?
(Repeat)

We're on our knees,
We're on our knees again.
We're on our knees,
We're on our knees again.

Let this nation be changed,
Let this nation be saved,
Let this nation be turned back to You.
(Repeat)

683

Matt Redman.

CAN I ASCEND the hill of the Lord?
Can I stand in that holy place?
There to approach the glory of my God;
Come towards to seek Your face.
Purify my heart,
And purify my hands,
For I know it is on holy ground I'll stand.

I'm coming up the mountain, Lord;
I'm seeking You and You alone.
I know that I will be transformed,

My heart unveiled before You.
I'm longing for Your presence, Lord;
Envelop me within the cloud.
I'm coming up the mountain, Lord,
My heart unveiled before You,
I will come.

I'm coming to worship,
I'm coming to bow down,
I'm coming to meet with You.
(Repeat)

684

Chris Bowater.

CATCH THE FIRE,
Swim through the waters,
Fly on the wings of the Spirit.
(Repeat)

Hear the sound that fills heaven,
Hear the beat of my heart.
(Repeat)

As a Lover, gazing on His bride;
As a Father looking for His child;
As the Shepherd,
Searching for the one that's lost;
As the Saviour, weeping for the world.

685

John L. Bell & Graham Maule.

CHRIST'S IS THE WORLD in which we move,
Christ's are the folk we're summoned to love,
Christ's is the voice which calls us to care,
And Christ is the One who calls us here.

To the lost Christ shows His face;
To the unloved He gives His embrace:
To those who cry in pain or disgrace,
Christ makes with His friends
A touching place.

Feel for the people we most avoid,
Strange or bereaved or never employed;
Feel for the women, and feel for the men
Who fear that their living is all in vain.

Feel for the parents who've lost their child,
Feel for the women whom men have defiled,
Feel for the baby for whom there's no breast,
And feel for the weary who find no rest.

Feel for the lives by life confused,
Riddled with doubt, in loving abused;
Feel for the lonely heart, conscious of sin,
Which longs to be pure but fears to begin.

686 Ian White.

CLAP YOUR HANDS, ALL YOU NATIONS,
Shout to God with cries of joy,
O how awesome is the Lord most high,
The King over all the earth!

He subdued nations under us,
The peoples under our feet,
And He chose our inheritance for us,
The pride of Jacob, whom He loved.

Now our God has ascended
In the midst of shouts of joy,
And the Lord is in among the trumpet sound,
Among the trumpet sound.

Sing praise to God,
Sing praises to the King,
Sing praises to the King.
(Repeat)

For our God is King of all the earth,
Sing Him a psalm of praise,
For He rules above the nations on His throne,
On His holy throne.

All the people are gathered
Of the God of Abraham.
For the kings of all the earth belong to God,
And He is lifted high!

687

Patricia Morgan.

CLOSER TO YOU, Lord, and closer still,
Till I am wholly in Your will.
Closer to hear Your beating heart,
And understand what You impart.
O Breath of Life, come purify
This heart of mine and satisfy.
My deep desire is to worship You,
Lord of my life, come closer still.

688

Valerie Collison.

COME AND JOIN THE CELEBRATION,
It's a very special day;
Come and share our jubilation,
There's a new King born today!

See the shepherds
Hurry down to Bethlehem;
Gaze in wonder
At the Son of God who lay before them.

Wise men journey,
Led to worship by a star,
Kneel in homage,
Bringing precious gifts from lands afar, so

'God is with us,'
'round the world the message bring;
He is with us,
'Welcome!' all the bells on earth are pealing.

689

Loralee Thiessen.

COME, HOLY SPIRIT,
Come, Holy Spirit,
Come to this place,
We will embrace Your presence.

Come, soften our hearts,
Come, soften our hearts,
That we may obey,
Teach us Your way, come lead us.

Come, Holy Spirit.
Come, Holy Spirit.

690

Billy Funk.

COME INTO THE HEAVENLIES
And sing the song the angels sing,
Worthy, worthy.
Come into the heavenlies,
And sing the song the angels sing,
Worthy, worthy.

Worthy is the Lamb.
Worthy is the Lamb.
Worthy is the Lamb.
Worthy is the Lamb.

Worthy of blessing and honour,
Worthy of glory and power,
Worthy is the Lamb.
(Repeat)

691

Kevin Prosch.

COME LET US RETURN unto the Lord.
(Men – Women echo)
Come let us return unto the Lord.
(Men – Women echo)
(Repeat)

For He has torn us,
But He will heal us.
For He has wounded us,
But He will bandage us.

And He will come,
He'll come to us
Like rain, spring rain.
He will come to us
Like rain, spring rain.

692

Graham Kendrick.

COME, LET US WORSHIP JESUS,
King of nations, Lord of all.
Magnificent and glorious,
Just and merciful.

Jesus, King of the nations,
Jesus, Lord of all.
Jesus, King of the nations,
Lord of all.

Lavish our hearts' affection,
Deepest love and highest praise.
Voice, race and language blending,
All the world amazed.

Bring tributes from the nations,
Come in joyful cavalcades,
One thunderous acclamation,
One banner raised.

Come, Lord, and fill Your temple,
Glorify Your dwelling place,
Till nations see Your splendour
And seek Your face.

Fear God and give Him glory,
For His hour of judgement comes.
Creator, Lord Almighty,
Worship Him alone.

693 John Pantry.

COME, MY SOUL, AND PRAISE THE LORD. *(Men – Women echo)*
Sing to Christ, the living Word, *(Men – Women echo)*
Who heals my broken heart, *(Men – Women echo)*
And binds my wounds. *(Men – Women echo)*

Holy, holy is the Lord, *(Men – Women echo)*
Who may stand before His word? *(Men – Women echo)*
He knows my life so well, *(Men – Women echo)*
Yet loves me still. *(Men – Women echo)*

As His eye is on the sparrow,
So His thoughts are for my life.
Not a moment passes by
But He thinks of me,
And He hears me when I cry.
So come my soul...

694

Noel Richards & Doug Horley.

COME OUT OF DARKNESS *into the light;*
Come out of darkness into the light.
Come out of darkness into the arms of love,
Into the arms of love.

To a world in darkness,
To a world in pain,
At this time You've called us,
Your love to proclaim;
Through Your willing people
To the nations say,
To the nations say:

Do not be discouraged,
See what God has done;
He is working through us,
This world shall be won.
There will be a harvest
When the nations hear.
What are they going to hear?

By the blood of Jesus sin is washed away;
All who call upon Him, He will surely save.
This will be the promise that the nations hear,
When we sing it loud and clear.

695

Richard Lewis.

COME TO THE POWER,
The power of the living God;
His name is higher,
Higher than any other name.
Mighty Jehovah, awesome Deliverer;
His power is greater,
Greater than any principality.

A mighty fortress is our God,
He sits enthroned in the heavens,
The Lord of Hosts is He.
A mighty fortress is our God,
He sits enthroned in the heavens,
He reigns in majesty.
(Repeat)
In majesty.

696

Chris Bowater.

CONFIDENCE, WE HAVE CONFIDENCE
To come, to ask for mercy.
Confidence, we have confidence,
To come, to ask for mercy.

Merciful God, we cry: 'Don't pass us by.'
Merciful God, we pray: 'Don't turn away;'
In Your love remember mercy.
In Your love remember mercy.

697

Geoff Bullock.

DAY BY DAY and hour by hour,
Your love for me from heaven flows;
Like streams of water in the desert,

Living waters flow.
You walk beside me, gently guiding,
Leading me through every storm.
Everlasting, never changing
Grace and love divine.

Mercy's healing grace, relieving
Every spot and every stain.
Forgiven freely, no more guilty,
Love has conquered shame.
The broken mended, night has ended,
Lost and lonely lost no more;
For I am carried in the arms of
Grace and love divine.

I am carried in the arms
Of grace and love divine;
I am held by hands of healing,
Washed by water pure;
Lifting up my heavy heart,
Held in grace scarred hands,
I am carried in the arms
Of grace and love divine.

Never worthy, never earning,
All my works now left behind.
Ever onwards, ever upwards,
You've called me on to rise
Above my darkness, all my failure,
Every fear and every pain.
Always carried, always covered by
Grace and love divine.

698

David Fellingham.

DAY OF FAVOUR, day of grace;
This is the day of jubilee.
The Spirit of the sovereign Lord

Is falling now on me.
Let the oil from heaven flow
From the presence of the King.
Jesus, let Your power flow
As we worship, as we sing.
Set us free to make You known
To a world that's full of shame.
Jesus, let Your glory fall,
Give us power to speak Your name.

Day of favour, day of grace;
This is the day of jubilee.
The Spirit of the sovereign Lord
Is falling now on me.
Open wide the prison doors,
Where satan's held the key.
Bring deliverance to the bound,
And set the captives free.
Bring the good news to the poor,
And cause the blind to see.
The Spirit of the Lord
Is falling now on me.

699

David Fellingham.

DAYS OF HEAVEN here on the earth;
Touched by power, touched by love.
By Your word, and by Your Spirit
You send Your blessing here on us.

Lord, send the rain,
Let Your Spirit come and glorify Jesus.
Lord, send the rain,
Let Your Spirit come like a pent up flood,
Driven by the breath of God.

We bring our worship, we see Your face;
We stand in wonder of Your grace.
Your kingdom presence, Your majesty;
Jesus, You're here now, hear our plea.

700

Martin Smith.

DID YOU FEEL THE MOUNTAINS TREMBLE?
Did you hear the oceans roar,
When the people rose to sing of
Jesus Christ, the risen One?

Did you feel the people tremble?
Did you hear the singers roar,
When the lost began to sing of
Jesus Christ, the saving One?

And we can see that God, You're moving,
A mighty river through the nations.
And young and old will turn to Jesus.
Fling wide you heavenly gates,
Prepare the way of the risen Lord.

Open up the doors
And let the music play,
Let the streets resound with singing.
Songs that bring Your hope,
Songs that bring Your joy,
Dancers who dance upon injustice.

Do you feel the darkness tremble,
When all the saints join in one song,
And all the streams flow as one river,
To wash away our brokenness?

And we can see that God, You're moving,
A time of jubilee is coming,
When young and old will turn to Jesus.
Fling wide you heavenly gates,
Prepare the way of the risen Lord.

701

Ian Smale.

DON'T BE LAZY,
Lazy, lazy, lazy,
But copy those who through faith and patience
Receive what God has promised.

702

Brian Doerksen.

DON'T LET MY LOVE GROW COLD;
I'm calling out, 'light the fire again.'
Don't let my vision die;
I'm calling out, 'light the fire again.'

You know my heart, my deeds;
I'm calling out, 'light the fire again.'
I need Your discipline;
I'm calling out, 'light the fire again.'

I am here to buy gold,
Refined in the fire:
Naked and poor,
Wretched and blind, I come.
Clothe me in white,
So I won't be ashamed:
Lord, light the fire again!

703

Andy Park.

DOWN THE MOUNTAIN THE RIVER FLOWS,
And it brings refreshing wherever it goes.
Through the valleys and over the fields,
The river is rushing and the river is here.

The river of God sets our feet a-dancing,
The river of God fills our hearts with cheer;
The river of God fills our mouths with laughter,
And we rejoice for the river is here.

The river God is teeming with life,
And all who touch it can be revived.
And those who linger on this river's shore
Will come back thirsting for more of the Lord.

Up to the mountain we love to go
To find the presence of the Lord.
Along the banks of the river we run,
We dance with laughter, giving praise to the Son.

704

Geoff & Judith Roberts.

DRAW ME CLOSE TO THE CROSS,
To the place of Your love,
To the place where You poured out Your mercy;
Where the river of life
That flows from Your wounded side
Brings refreshing to those who draw near.
Draw me close to Your throne
Where Your majesty is shown,
Where the crown of my life I lay down.
Draw me close to Your side,
Where my heart is satisfied,
Draw me close to You, Lord,
Draw me close.

705

David Fellingham.

ETERNAL COVENANT of God
Down through time has been declared;
Drawing the heart of man
Into redemption's plan,
Mercy and grace revealed,
By the blood and Spirit sealed.
All our sins have been forgiven,
Raised from death to heights of heaven.

And we're living to the praise of His glory,
Eternally secure in His love;
The eyes of our hearts have been opened
To receive the blessing of God.
(Repeat)

706

Dave Bilbrough.

FAITHFUL AND TRUE
Are all Your ways;
Your love for me will never fade away.
Always the same,
You never change;
Your love for me will never fade away.

Even in my hour of deepest need,
You are always there to walk with me.
You know my words before I speak;
Lord, I know that You will never forsake me.

707

Chris Bowater.

FAITHFUL GOD, faithful God,
All sufficient One, I worship You.
Shalom my peace,
My strong Deliverer,
I lift You up, faithful God.

708

David Fellingham.

FAR ABOVE ALL OTHER LOVES,
Far beyond all other joys,
Heaven's blessings poured on me,
By the Holy Spirit's power.

Love's compelling power
Draws my heart into Yours;
Jesus, how I love You,
You're my Friend and my Lord.
You have died and risen
So what else can I say?
How I love You, Lord,
Love You, Lord.

All ambition now has gone,
Pleasing You my only goal;
Motivated by Your grace,
Living for eternity.

Looking with the eye of faith
For the day of Your return;
In that day I want to stand
Unashamed before Your throne.

709

Graham Kendrick.

FAR AND NEAR hear the call,
Worship Him, Lord of all;
Families of nations come,
Celebrate what God has done.

Deep and wide is the love
Heaven sent from above;
God's own Son for sinners died,
Rose again, He is alive.

Say it loud, say it strong,
Tell the world what God has done;
Say it loud, praise His name,
Let the earth rejoice
For the Lord reigns.

At His name let praise begin,
Oceans roar, nature sing.
For He comes to judge the earth
In righteousness and in His truth.

710

Dave Bilbrough.

FATHER GOD, fill this place
With Your love, with Your grace.
As we call on Your name,
Visit us in power again.

Lord, we worship You.
Lord, we worship You.
(Repeat)

Spirit come with Your peace;
Heal our wounds, bring release.
Lord we long for Your touch,
Fill our hearts with Your love.

711

John Barnett.

FATHER, I COME TO YOU, lifting up my hands
In the name of Jesus, by Your grace I stand.
Just because You love me and I love Your Son,
I know Your favour, unending love.

I receive Your favour, Your unending love,
Not because I've earned it, not for what I've done;
Just because You love me and I love Your Son,
I know Your favour, unending love.

Unending love,
Your unending love.

It's the presence of Your kingdom as Your glory fills this place,
And I see how much You love me as I look into Your face.
Nothing could be better, there's nothing I would trade
For Your favour, unending love.

712

Jim Bailey.

FATHER IN HEAVEN, holy is Your name.
Your kingdom come, Your will be done,
Let it be the same.
(Repeat)
On earth as it is in heaven,
On earth as it is in heaven.
(Repeat)

Give us today all our daily bread,
As we forgive our debtors,
So You forgive our debts.
(Repeat)
And lead us not into temptation;
Deliver us from evil.
(Repeat)

For Yours is the kingdom,
The power and the glory,
Forever and ever and ever, amen.
(Repeat)

713

Paul McWilliams & William Thompson.

FATHER, LIKE RAIN FROM THE SKIES,
Send Your word into our lives.
We cry out: 'Show us Your way,
Come to us, Father, we pray.'

Come and satisfy,
Come and satisfy my soul.
Come and satisfy,
Come and satisfy my soul
And make me whole.

When will our hearts understand,
You have our lives in Your hand?
We cry out: 'Come to us, Lord,
Guide us we pray with Your word.'

714

David Ruis.

FATHER OF CREATION,
Unfold Your sovereign plan.
Raise up a chosen generation
That will march through the land.
All of creation is longing
For Your unveiling of power.
Would You release Your anointing;
O God, let this be the hour.

Let Your glory fall in this room,
Let it go forth from here to the nations.
Let Your fragrance rest in this place,
As we gather to seek Your face.

Ruler of the nations,
The world has yet to see
The full release of Your promise,
The church in victory.
Turn to us, Lord, and touch us,
Make us strong in Your might.
Overcome our weakness,
That we could stand up and fight.

(Men) Let Your kingdom come.
(Women) Let Your kingdom come.
(Men) Let Your will be done.
(Women) Let Your will be done.
(Men) Let us see on earth
(Women) Let us see on earth
(All) The glory of Your Son.

715

Robert Critchley.

FATHER, YOU HAVE GIVEN
Precious gifts from heaven,
Equipping us to serve You
As You move upon the earth.
You've prepared us for this hour,
And anointed us with power
For humble acts of righteousness,
We freely volunteer to do Your work.

Ambassadors of reconciliation,
Preaching the good news of Jesus Christ;
Praying for the increase of Your kingdom,
Piercing the darkness with Your light.

Not to us, but to You be all the praises,
Not to us, but to the glory of Your grace.
We will lift up a standard to this world,
Not for us, but for the honour of Your name.
Oh, Father, not for us,
But for the honour of Your name.

For the honour of Your name.
Oh, Your name.
(Repeat)

Father, You have chosen
The weak and the broken,
These ones are the vessels
Through whom You command Your strength.
We offer up our lives as living sacrifices,
Fill us with Your Spirit now,
And send us out to bring the harvest in.

Ambassadors of reconciliation...

716

Noel & Tricia Richards.

FILLED WITH COMPASSION for all creation,
Jesus came into a world that was lost.
There was but one way that He could save us,
Only through suffering death on a cross.

God, You are waiting,
Your heart is breaking
For all the people who live on the earth.
Stir us to action,
Filled with Your passion
For all the people who live on the earth.

Great is Your passion for all the people
Living and dying without knowing You.
Having no Saviour, they're lost forever,
If we don't speak out and lead them to You.

From every nation we shall be gathered,
Millions redeemed shall be Jesus' reward.
Then He will turn and say to His Father:
'Truly my suffering was worth it all.'

717

Timothy Dudley-Smith.

FILL YOUR HEARTS WITH JOY and gladness,
Sing and praise your God and mine!
Great the Lord in love and wisdom,
Might and majesty divine!
He who framed the starry heavens
Knows and names them as they shine.

Praise the Lord, His people, praise Him!
Wounded souls His comfort know;
Those who fear Him find His mercies,
Peace for pain and joy for woe;
Humble hearts are high exalted,
Human pride and power laid low.

Praise the Lord for times and seasons,
Cloud and sunshine, wind and rain;
Spring to melt the snows of winter
Till the waters flow again;
Grass upon the mountain pastures,
Golden valleys thick with grain.

Fill your hearts with joy and gladness,
Peace and plenty crown your days;
Love His laws, declare His judgements,
Walk in all His words and ways;
He the Lord and we His children –
Praise the Lord, all people, praise!

718

Paul Oakley.

FIRE, *there's a fire,*
Sweet fire burning in my heart.
(Repeat)

And I will run with all of the passion
You've put in me.
I will spread the seed of the gospel everywhere.

And I can feel the power of Your hand upon me.
Now I know I'll never be the same again.
For as long as You will give me breath,
My heart is so resolved,
Oh, to lay my life before You, Lord,
Let everything I do be to Your praise.

Let me feel Your tongues of fire resting upon me;
Let me hear the sound of
Your mighty rushing wind.
Let my life be like an offering of worship;
Let me be a living sacrifice of praise.

719

Ian Smale.

5000+ HUNGRY FOLK,
5000+ hungry folk,
5000+ hungry folk
Came 4 2 listen 2 Jesus.

The 6 x 2 said 0 0 0,
The 6 x 2 said 0 0 0,
The 6 x 2 said 0 0 0,
Where can I get some food from?

Just 1 had 1 2 3 4 5,
Just 1 had 1 2 3 4 5,
Just 1 had 1 2 3 4 5,
Loaves and 1 2 fishes.

When Jesus blessed the 5 + 2,
When Jesus blessed the 5 + 2,
When Jesus blessed the 5 + 2,
They were increased many x over.

5000 + 8 it up,
5000 + 8 it up,
5000 + 8 it up,
With 1 2 3 4 5 6 7 8 9 10 11 12 basketfuls left over.

720

Ian White.

FOCUS MY EYES on You, O Lord,
Focus my eyes on You;
To worship in spirit and in truth,
Focus my eyes on You.

Turn round my life to You, O Lord,
Turn round my life to You;
To know from this night You've made me new,
Turn round my life to You.

Fill up my heart with praise, O Lord,
Fill up my heart with praise;
To speak of Your love in every place,
Fill up my heart with praise.

721

Graham Kendrick.

FOR THE JOYS AND FOR THE SORROWS,
The best and worst of times,
For this moment, for tomorrow,
For all that lies behind;
Fears that crowd around me,
For the failure of my plans,
For the dreams of all I hope to be,
The truth of what I am:

For this I have Jesus,
For this I have Jesus,
For this I have Jesus,
I have Jesus.
(Repeat)

For the tears that flow in secret,
In the broken times,
For the moments of elation,
Or the troubled mind;
For all the disappointments,
Or the sting of old regrets,
All my prayers and longings
That seem unanswered yet:

For the weakness of my body,
The burdens of each day,
For the nights of doubt and worry,
When sleep has fled away;
Needing reassurance,
And the will to start again,
A steely-eyed endurance,
The strength to fight and win:

722

Matt Redman.

FRIEND OF SINNERS, Lord of truth,
I am falling in love with You.
Friend of sinners, Lord of truth,
I have fallen in love with You.

Jesus, I love Your name,
The name by which we're saved.
Jesus, I love Your name,
The name by which we're saved.

Friend of sinners, Lord of truth,
I am giving my life to You.
Friend of sinners, Lord of truth,
I have given my life to You.

723

Wayne Drain.

FROM EVERY TONGUE, tribe and nation,
Shouted out from all creation,
All the earth sings forth Your praise.
Even the trees clap their hands,
As the people of God take their stand,
Jesus Christ our banner we raise.

You're our God, our heart's desire,
Breathe on our lives, release Your power.
Deep in our hearts we already know
That we'll be set free when we give up control.
Yeah, we'll be set free when we give up control.

In every circumstance or situation
We give thanks and adoration,
Jesus Christ is worthy of praise.
Whenever our minds give in to fear and doubting,
Feeling alone or left out,
We lift our hands and we start to sing.

724 Stuart Townend.

La la la la la la. (x4)

FROM THE SLEEP OF AGES,
I am stirred by the kiss of love,
By the fragrant perfume
When His name is mentioned.
I have learned to wait for Him,
To receive His presence
With the sound of laughter,
And the joy of resting.
But listen, my Lover
Is coming from heaven's throne!

Over the mountains, leaping the hills,
He runs like a deer through the open plain;
Gazing through windows,
Peering through doors,
My Lover is calling and calling again:
'Rise up, my lovely, beautiful one,
The winter is past and the rains are gone;
Flowers appear all over the earth,
These are the promised days.'
This is the season of singing. (x4)

There is no preferring
In the Lover's loving;
We are all His treasure,
His desired inheritance.
He has come with blessings
From the Father's throne-room;
Gifts of power and healing,
For a needy people.
The wonder, the pleasure
Of knowing, of being known!

725

Chris Cartwright.

FROM YOUR THRONE, O LORD,
Let Your fire fall upon us;
Let us feel the touch of the Spirit in our hearts,
To equip us and empower us,
Send us out to heal the land,
In Your name to shine the light of Christ.

From the Father's heart
Send us waves of Your compassion;
Move us, Lord, to pray for
Your will to come on earth.
Interceding for a nation
That is dying, lost and blind,
Let us see them with the eyes of Christ.

Lord, we lift one voice
In a song of joy and triumph;
Let Your word rise up from our lips, that in our lives
We will let the world know Jesus
Is the Victor and the King,
Let our anthem ring throughout the land.

726

Jim Bailey.

GIVE ME A HEART OF COMPASSION,
Give me a hope for the lost.
Give me a passion for those
Who are broken and down.
Lord, I am ready and willing
To serve the weak and the young;
Help me to put into action
The words of this song.

And enable Your servants,
Enable Your servants
To preach good news,
To preach good news.
(Repeat)

I'll sing the songs of salvation,
Boldly I'll speak out Your word.
I'll let them know by my life,
I will show You are Lord.
I'll tell them all about Jesus,
I'll tell them all about You;
I'm not ashamed of the gospel
Or what it can do.

We're moving forward together,
As one voice boldly proclaim
The old and the young will be strong,
And we'll lift up Your name
On to the streets to the people,
Every man, woman and child,
And as we go You are with us,
You've given Your power.

You've enabled Your servants...

727

Dave Bilbrough.

GIVE ME, LORD, A DREAM FROM HEAVEN,
Let me see the things You see;
Give me purpose and direction,
Holy Spirit, move on me.
I would set my face to serve You,
To do the things You'd have me do;
Stir within my heart a vision,
Lord, I will follow You.

By Your Spirit and Your word,
We would hasten Your return.
(Repeat)

Give to me a holy passion,
With every breath I will proclaim
The message of Your kingdom,
The glory of Your name.
Lead me into action,
Let me do the things You say;
Send me to the nations,
When You speak I will obey.

I believe that faith is rising,
I can see a tidal wave
Of Your Spirit that is moving
To end this final age.
There'll be shouts of acclamation
When You come back for Your Bride;
History's consummation
Is here before our eyes.

728

Author unknown.

GIVE ME OIL IN MY LAMP, keep me burning.
Give me oil in my lamp, I pray.
Give me oil in my lamp, keep my burning,
Keep me burning till the break of day.

Sing hosanna, sing hosanna,
Sing hosanna to the King of kings.
Sing hosanna, sing hosanna,
Sing hosanna to the King.

Give me joy in my heart, keep me praising…

Give me peace in my heart, keep me resting…

Give me love in my heart, keep me serving…

729

Dave Bilbrough.

GIVE YOUR THANKS TO THE RISEN SON.
(Leader – all echo)
To the holy and anointed one. *(echo)*
Who fills our hearts with a joyful song. *(echo)*
Jesus. *(echo)*

Turn to Him, don't be afraid,
Give Him honour, give Him praise.
Lift Him up to the highest place.
Jesus.

Worship Him, crown Him King,
And give Him all your heart.
(Repeat)

730

Graham Kendrick & Steve Thompson.

GOD IS GREAT, *amazing!*
Come, let His praises ring.
God is great, astounding!
The whole creation sings.

His clothing is splendour and majesty bright,
For He wraps Himself in a garment of light.
He spreads out the heavens – His palace of stars,
And rides on the wings of the wind.

What marvellous wisdom the Maker displays,
The sea vast and spacious, the dolphins and whales,
The earth full of creatures, the great and the small,
He watches and cares for them all.

The rain forest canopies darken the skies,
Cathedrals of mist that resound with the choirs,
Of creatures discordant, outrageous, ablaze
In colourful pageants of praise.

Above His creation the Father presides:
The pulse of the planets, the rhythm of tides,
The moon makes the seasons, the day follows night,
Yet He knows every beat of my heart.

Let cannons of thunder salute their acclaim,
The sunsets fly glorious banners of flame,
The angels shout 'holy' again and again
As they soar in the arch of the heavens.

731

Jim Bailey.

GOD IS RAISING UP AN ARMY
Made of those who are still young.
God is lifting up their voices,
Through the weak He'll shame the strong.
It's been prophesied they will prophesy,
God's salvation they will show;
For the promise is to the children,
To our daughters and our sons.

Children of the cross,
A shining example,
Children of the cross
Are singing His praise.
Children of the cross
Are silencing the enemy,
Children of the cross
Are saying the Lord saves.

732

Author unknown.

GOD IS SO GOOD,
God is so good,
God is so good,
He's so good to me.

He took my sin,
He took my sin,
He took my sin,
He's so good to me.

Now I am free,
Now I am free,
Now I am free,
He's so good to me.

God is so good,
He took my sin,
Now I am free,
He's so good to me.

733

Kevin Prosch.

(And) **GOD IS SO GOOD.**
(And) God is so good.

He rides upon the wings of the wind,
He is exalted by His name Jah.
He walks in the midst of the stones of fire,
To be His sons is our desire.
For the natural things speak of the invisible.
Look around and see,
Who could deny the wonders of His love?

You reign on high in majesty,
And the widow's heart causes to sing.
You hear the cry of the fatherless,
And the depths of Your love who can comprehend?
For the natural things speak of the invisible.
Look around and see,
Who could deny the wonders of His love?

734

Stuart Townend.

GOD OF HEAVEN, with the heart of a lover;
Conquering King, with compassion in His voice.
Sovereign Lord, with the care of a mother;
To You we bring our lives, knowing You will take us in.

Jesus Christ, You're the Alpha and Omega:
King of kings, who laid aside His crown.
Man of woes, but a Friend to the friendless:
To You we bring our fears, knowing You will set us free.

So let's be pure and holy, set apart for Jesus;
A covenant people, who reflect the heart of God.
With outstretched hands of mercy to the broken-hearted,
A covenant people who reveal the love of God.

735

Rosie Fellingham.

GOD, OUR GOD, BLESSES US,
God blesses us,
That all the ends of the earth may fear Him.
(Repeat)

Let all the peoples praise Thee, O God,
Let all the peoples praise Him.

736

Gloria & William J Gaither.

GOD SENT HIS SON, they called Him Jesus;
He came to love, heal, and forgive;
He lived and died to buy my pardon,
An empty grave is there to prove my Saviour lives.

Because He lives I can face tomorrow;
Because He lives all fear is gone;
Because I know He holds the future,
And life is worth the living
Just because He lives.

How sweet to hold a new-born baby,
And feel the pride and joy he gives;
But greater still the calm assurance,
This child can face uncertain days because He lives.

And then one day I'll cross the river;
I'll fight life's final war with pain;
And then as death gives way to victory,
I'll see the lights of glory and I'll know He lives.

737

Charlotte Exon & Andy Thorpe.

GOD, YOU ARE AN AWESOME GOD,
And Your dominion reaches to the heavens,
And all nations sing Your praise;
As Your people, we declare Your holiness.

Holy, holy, holy is the Lord.
Holy, holy, holy is the Lord.

738

James E. Seddon.

GO FORTH AND TELL! O Church of God, awake!
God's saving news to all the nations take:
Proclaim Christ Jesus, Saviour, Lord and King,
That all the world His worthy praise may sing.

Go forth and tell! God's love embraces all;
He will in grace respond to all who call:
How shall they call if they have never heard
The gracious invitation of His word?

Go forth and tell where still the darkness lies,
In wealth or want, the sinner surely dies;
Give us, O Lord, concern of heart and mind,
A love like Yours, compassionate and kind.

Go forth and tell! The doors are open wide:
Share God's good gifts – let no one be denied;
Live out your life as Christ your Lord shall choose,
Your ransomed powers for His sole glory use.

Go forth and tell! O church of God, arise!
Go in the strength which Christ your Lord supplies;
Go till all nations His great name adore
And serve Him, Lord and King forever more.

739

Graham Kendrick.

GOOD NEWS, GOOD NEWS TO YOU WE BRING,
Alleluia!
News of great joy that angels sing,
Alleluia!

Tender mercy He has shown us,
Joy to all the world;
For us God sends His only Son,
Alleluia!

Let earth's dark shadows fly away,
Alleluia!
In Christ has dawned an endless day,
Alleluia!

Now God with us on earth resides,
Alleluia!
And heaven's door is open wide,
Alleluia!

740

Bryn Haworth.

GO TO ALL NATIONS, making disciples,
Baptising them in My name.
Go to all nations, making disciples,
Baptising them in My name.

I am coming soon.
I am coming soon.
I'm waiting at the gates
For the Father's call.
I am coming soon.
Yes, I am coming soon.

Teach them to do all I told you to do,
Teach them to walk in My ways.
I have authority in heaven and earth,
I will be with you always.

741

Doug Horley.

Oh, it's **GREAT, GREAT, BRILL, BRILL,**
Wicked, wicked, skill, skill,
To have a friend like Jesus.
Great, great, brill, brill,
Wicked, wicked, skill, skill,
To have a friend like Him.
(Repeat)

He's always there,
He always listens,
He always hears me when I talk to Him.
He loves me now
And will forever,
I'll choose Him every day, day, day.

742

GREAT IS THE DARKNESS that covers the earth,
Oppression, injustice and pain.
Nations are slipping in hopeless despair,
Though many have come in Your name.
Watching while sanity dies,
Touched by the madness and lies.

Come, Lord Jesus, come, Lord Jesus,
Pour out Your Spirit we pray.
Come, Lord Jesus, come, Lord Jesus,
Pour out Your Spirit on us today.

May now Your church rise with power and love,
This glorious gospel proclaim.
In every nation salvation will come
To those who believe in Your name.
Help us bring light to this world
That we might speed Your return.

Great celebrations on that final day
When out of the heavens You come.
Darkness will vanish, all sorrow will end,
And rulers will bow at Your throne.
Our great commission complete,
Then face to face we shall meet.

743

GREAT IS THE LORD;
Sovereign King,
We give You praise.

You spoke Your word and You rescued me,
You poured out Your grace and You set me free.
Now You've filled my life with the Spirit's power,
And You've set my heart on fire.

And by the power of Jesus' name
You have raised me up from my sin and shame.
You've anointed me with the Spirit's power,
And You've set my heart on fire.

By grace I'm saved through faith in God,
Not by works alone but by Jesus' blood.
Now I'm filled with strength by the Spirit's power,
And You've set my heart on fire.

Great is the Lord.
(Repeat)

744

Ron Kenoly.

HALLELUJAH! JESUS IS ALIVE,
Death has lost its victory
And the grave has been denied;
Jesus lives forever,
He's alive, He's alive!
(Last time)
Hallelujah! Jesus is alive!

He's the Alpha and Omega,
The First and Last is He;
The curse of sin is broken
And we have perfect liberty.
The Lamb of God has risen,
He's alive, He's alive!

745

Doug Horley.

HANDS, HANDS, FINGERS, THUMBS,
We can lift to praise You.
Hands, hands, fingers, thumbs,
We can lift to praise.
Hands, hands, fingers, thumbs,
We can lift to praise You.
Jump front, jump back, yeah!
We were made to praise.

We've got some hands that we can raise.
We've got a voice to shout Your praise, Jesus!
Got some feet a-made to dance;
Let's use them now we've got the chance.
(Repeat)

We were made to praise You,
We were made to praise.
We were made to praise You,
We were made to praise.
(Repeat)

746

Mick Gisbey.

HAVE YOU GOT AN APPETITE?
Do you eat what is right?
Are you feeding on the word of God?
Are you fat or are you thin?
Are you really full within?
Do you find your strength in Him or are you starving?

You and me all should be
Exercising regularly,
Standing strong all day long,
Giving God the glory.

Feeding on the living Bread,
Not eating crumbs but loaves instead;
Standing stronger, living longer,
Giving God the glory.

If it's milk or meat you need,
Why not have a slap-up feed,
And stop looking like a weed and start to grow?
Take the full of fitness food,
Taste and see that God is good,
Come on, feed on what you should and be healthy.

747 Stuart Garrard.

HAVE YOU HEARD THE GOOD NEWS?
Have you heard the good news?
We can live in hope
Because of what the Lord has done.
(Repeat)

There is a way
When there seems to be no way,
There is a light in the darkness:
There is a hope,
An everlasting hope,
There is a God who can help us.

A hope for justice
And a hope for peace,
A hope for those in desperation:
We have a future,
If only we believe
He works in every situation.

748

Matt Redman.

HAVE YOU NOT SAID as we pass through water,
You will be with us?
And You have said as we walk through fire,
We will not be burned.
We are not afraid, for You are with us;
We will testify to the honour of Your name.
We are witnesses, You have shown us
You are the One who can save.

Fill us up and send us out
In the power of Your name.
Fill us up and send us out
In the power of Your name.

Bring them from the west, sons and daughters,
Call them for Your praise.
Gather from the east all Your children,
Coming home again.
Bring them from afar, all the nations,
From the north and south,
Drawing all the peoples in.
Corners of the earth, come to see there's
Only one Saviour and King.

749

Russell Fragar.

HEAR THESE PRAISES FROM A GRATEFUL HEART,
Each time I think of You the praises start:
Love You so much, Jesus,
Love You so much.

Lord I love You, my soul sings,
In Your presence, carried on Your wings:
Love You so much, Jesus,
Love You so much.

How my soul longs for You,
Longs to worship You forever
In Your power and majesty.
Lift my hands, lift my heart,
Lift my voice towards the heavens,
For You are my sun and shield.

750 Kevin Prosch.

HE BROUGHT ME TO HIS BANQUETING TABLE,
(Men-Women echo)
He brought me to His banqueting table, *(Men-Women echo)*
And His banner over me is love. *(All)*

I am my Belovèd's and He is mine, *(Men-Women echo)*
I am my Belovèd's and He is mine, *(Men-Women echo)*
And His banner over me is love. *(All)*
Yes, His banner over me is love.

And we can feel the love of God in this place,
We believe Your goodness, we receive Your grace.
We delight ourselves at Your table, O God,
You do all things well, just look at our lives.

751 David Fellingham.

HE HAS BEEN GIVEN a Name above all names,
In earth and heaven, let all creation claim
That Jesus Christ is King, and Lord of all.

He is the Victor over satan's reign,
His blood has triumphed over sin and shame,
Jesus Christ is King and Lord of all.

He is the likeness of Jehovah,
Through whom the world was made.
By His word the universe is sustained,
Every power is subject to His name.

The name of Jesus in victory will resound,
In every nation let the good news sound:
Jesus Christ is King, and Lord of all.

752

Steve & Vikki Cook.

HE HAS CLOTHED US WITH HIS RIGHTEOUSNESS,
Covered us with His great love.
He has showered us with mercy,
And we delight to know the glorious favour,
Wondrous favour of God.

We rejoice in the grace of God
Poured upon our lives.
Loving kindness has come to us
Because of Jesus Christ.
We rejoice in the grace of God,
Our hearts overflow.
What a joy to know the grace of God!

He's brought us into His family,
Made us heirs with His own Son.
All good things He freely gives us,
And we cannot conceive what God's preparing
God's preparing for us.

753

HE HAS RISEN,
He has risen,
He has risen,
Jesus is alive.

When the life flowed from His body,
Seemed like Jesus' mission failed.
But His sacrifice accomplished,
Victory over sin and hell.

In the grave God did not leave Him,
For His body to decay;
Raised to life, the great awakening,
Satan's power He overcame.

If there were no resurrection,
We ourselves could not be raised;
But the Son of God is living,
So our hope is not in vain.

When the Lord rides out of heaven,
Mighty angels at His side,
They will sound the final trumpet,
From the grave we shall arise.

He has given life immortal,
We shall see Him face to face;
Through eternity we'll praise Him,
Christ, the Champion of our faith.

754

HE IS LOVELY, *He is holy,*
Gave supremely, that all men may see.
He is gentle, tender-hearted,
Risen Saviour, He is God.

Master, Maker, Life Creator,
Come and dwell in me,
That my heart may know
Your tender mercy.
Shine through me that all may see
Your love so full and free;
And I'll declare Your praise
Through endless ages.

755

Kevin Prosch.

HE IS THE LORD, and He reigns on high:
He is the Lord.
Spoke into the darkness, created the light:
He is the Lord.
Who is like unto Him, never ending in days?
He is the Lord.
And He comes in power when we call on His name:
He is the Lord.

Show Your power, O Lord our God.
Show Your power, O Lord our God,
Our God.

Your gospel, O Lord, is the hope for our nation:
You are the Lord.
It's the power of God for our salvation:
You are the Lord.
We ask not for riches, but look to the cross:
You are the Lord.
And for our inheritance give us the lost:
You are the Lord.

Send Your power . . .

756

HE MADE THE EARTH, He made the sky,
He made the moon and the stars,
Jupiter and Mars.
He made the sun for everyone,
Our God made them all.
Our God is powerful, powerful,
Our God is great.
Our God is powerful, powerful,
Our God is great.

He made the fish, He made the birds,
Elephants and worms,
Creeping things that squirm.
Mice so small, giraffes so tall;
Our God made them all.
Our God is wonderful, wonderful,
Our God is great.
Our God is wonderful, wonderful,
Our God is great.

He made the boys, he made the girls,
He made our mums and dads,
To teach us good from bad.
He cares for me, He cares for You;
Our God loves us all.
Our God is beautiful, beautiful,
Our God is great.
Our God is beautiful, beautiful,
Our God is great.

757

Dave Bilbrough.

HE PICKED ME UP
And He dusted me down,
Put my feet back on solid ground.
He welcomed me home
And He caused me to sing,
I'm in love, I'm in love with the King.

For all my days I'll sing His praise,
I'm so grateful.
Yes, I will give my everything
To the One who sets me free.

Once I was lost, but now I'm found,
Yes, He saved me.
He called my name and my life was changed
By the power of His love.

758

Paul Oakley.

HERE I AM, and I have come
To thank You, Lord, for all You've done;
Thank You, Lord.
You paid the price at Calvary,
You shed Your blood, You set me free;
Thank You, Lord.
No greater love was ever shown,
No better life ever was laid down.

And I will always love Your name;
And I will always sing Your praise.
(Repeat)

You took my sin, You took my shame,
You drank my cup, You bore my pain;
Thank You, Lord.
You broke the curse, You broke the chains,
In victory from death You rose again;
Thank You, Lord.
And not by works, but by Your grace
You clothe me now in Your righteousness.

You bid me come, You make me whole,
You give me peace, You restore my soul;
Thank You, Lord.
You fill me up, and when I'm full,
You give me more till I overflow;
Thank You, Lord.
You're making me to be like You,
To do the works of the Father, too.

759

Craig Musseau.

HERE I AM ONCE AGAIN,
I pour out my heart for I know that You hear
Every cry; You are listening,
No matter what state my heart is in.

You are faithful to answer
With words that are true
And a hope that is real.
As I feel Your touch,
You bring a freedom to all that's within.

In the safety of this place
I'm longing to...

Pour out my heart, to say that I love You,
Pour out my heart, to say that I need You.
Pour out my heart, to say that I'm thankful,
Pour out my heart, to say that You're wonderful.

760 Rick Ridings.

HE REIGNS, *He reigns, Jesus reigns,*
He reigns enthroned in majesty.
Shout your praise, His banners raise,
For Jesus reigns.
Shout hosanna, Jesus reigns.

Our highest praise we bring
To our great eternal King.
His glory fills the skies,
Now from earth let praise arise.

He spoiled the hosts of hell,
And like blazing stars, they fell.
He led them forth in chains—
Now our mighty Victor reigns!

761 Chris Bowater.

HERE IN THE PRESENCE of the
Great and awesome God.
Here in the presence of the Holy One,
The only One.
Knowing not how best to bring adoring love,
To bow, to weep, to fall, and yet
You whisper, 'Child, draw near:

And stand in the presence of the Lord,
Stand in the presence of the Lord,
Stand in the presence of the Holy One,
Stand in the presence of the Lord.'

Here in the presence of the
Great and awesome God,
Majestic in His power yet full of grace:
I seek His face.

The passion in His eyes
Searches deep inside:
Such shining love intensifies,
Yet melts away my fears.

And I stand...

762

Graham Kendrick.

HERE IS BREAD, here is wine,
Christ is with us – He is with us;
Break the bread, drink the wine –
Christ is with us here.

Here is grace, here is peace,
Christ is with us – He is with us;
Know His grace, find His peace –
Feast on Jesus here.

In this bread there is healing,
In this cup there's life forever;
In this moment, by the Spirit
Christ is with us here.

Here we are, joined in one,
Christ is with us – He is with us;
We'll proclaim, till He comes –
Jesus crucified.

763

Michael Sandeman.

HERE IS THE RISEN SON,
Riding out in glory,
Radiating light all around.
Here is the Holy Spirit,
Poured out for the nations,
Glorifying Jesus the Lamb.

We will stand as a people
Who are upright and holy,
We will worship the Lord of hosts.
We will watch, we will wait
On the walls of the city,
We will look and see what He will say to us.

Every knee shall bow before Him,
Every tongue confess
That He is King of kings, Lord of lords,
And Ruler of the earth.

764

HERE WE ARE, LORD,
More weak than strong;
Still believing, still pressing on.
Make us ready
With hearts that are brave.
We will silence the lies of this age.

For such a moment we have been born.
We're gonna rise up,
Take this world by storm.
Let evil tremble,
We come in His name.
Our God is with us,
We're dangerous people.

All God's heroes failed as we do,
Sometimes doubting all that is true.
Yet He calls us great people of faith,
Working through us as history is made.

765

Charlie Groves and Andy Piercy.

HERE WE STAND IN TOTAL SURRENDER,
Lifting our voices, abandoned to Your cause.
Here we stand, praying in the glory
Of the one and only Jesus Christ, the Lord.

This time revival!
Lord, come and heal our land;
Bring to completion
The work that You've begun.
This time revival!
Stir up Your church again,
Pour out Your Spirit
On Your daughters and Your sons.

Here we stand in need of Your mercy;
Father, forgive us for the time that we have lost.
Once again make us an army
To conquer this nation with the message of the cross.

766

David Ruis.

HIS LOVE is higher than the highest of mountains.
His love goes deeper that the deepest of seas.
His love, it stretches to the farthest horizon,
And His love, it reaches to me.

His love is stronger than the angels and demons.
His love, it keeps me in my life's darkest hour.
His love secures me on the pathway to heaven,
And His love is my strength and power.

His love is sweeter than the sweetest of honey.
His love is better than the choicest of wine.
His love, it satisfies the deepest of hunger,
And His love, in Jesus it's mine.

Your love is higher…

767 Noel & Tricia Richards.

HOLD ME CLOSER TO YOU EACH DAY;
May my love for You never fade.
Keep my focus on all that's true;
May I never lose sight of You.

In my failure, in my success,
If in sadness or happiness,
Be the hope I am clinging to,
For my heart belongs to You.

You are only a breath away,
Watching over me every day;
In my heart I am filled with peace
When I hear You speak to me.

No one loves me the way You do,
No one cares for me like You do.
Feels like heaven has broken through;
God, You know how I love You.

768 Brian Doerksen.

HOLINESS IS YOUR LIFE IN ME,
Making me clean through Your blood.
Holiness is Your fire in me,
Purging my heart like a flood.
I know You are perfect in holiness.
Your life in me, setting me free,
Making me holy.

Only the blood of Jesus covers all of my sin.
Only the life of Jesus renews me from within.
Your blood is enough, Your mercy complete.
Your work of atonement, paid for my debts,
Making me holy.
Only the blood of Jesus.

769 Timothy Dudley-Smith.

HOLY CHILD, how still You lie!
Safe the manger, soft the hay;
Faint upon the eastern sky
Breaks the dawn of Christmas Day.

Holy Child, whose birthday brings
Shepherds from their field and fold,
Angel choirs and eastern kings,
Myrrh and frankincense and gold:

Holy Child, what gift of grace
From the Father freely willed!
In Your infant form we trace
All God's promises fulfilled.

Holy Child, whose human years
Span like ours delight and pain;
One in human joys and tears,
One in all but sin and stain:

Holy Child, so far from home,
All the lost to seek and save:
To what dreadful death You come,
To what dark and silent grave!

Holy Child, before whose name
Powers of darkness faint and fall;
Conquered death and sin and shame –
Jesus Christ is Lord of all!

Holy Child, how still You lie!
Safe the manger, soft the hay;
Clear upon the eastern sky
Breaks the dawn of Christmas Day.

770 Bjorn Aslakson.

HOLY GHOST,
You wonderful Holy Ghost,
A wind blowing strong,
Blowing from heaven.
(Repeat)

We have decided to go
All the way with our God.
Revival in the land, that's our goal;
As soldiers in His army
We'll fight with heart and soul.

(Final chorus)
Blood and fire,
We call upon blood and fire,
A wind blowing strong,
Blowing from heaven.
(Repeat)

771 Nathan Fellingham.

HOLY, HOLY,
Holy is the Lord God Almighty.
(Repeat)
Who was and is and is to come,
Who was and is and is to come.

Lift up His name with the sound of singing,
Lift up His name in all the earth.
Lift up your voice and give Him glory,
For He is worthy to be praised.

772

Jimmy Owens.

HOLY, HOLY, HOLY, HOLY,
Holy, holy, Lord God Almighty!
And we lift our hearts before You
As a token of our love:
Holy, holy, holy, holy.

Gracious Father, gracious Father,
We're so glad to be Your children, gracious Father;
And we lift our heads before You
As a token of our love,
Gracious Father, gracious Father.

Precious Jesus, precious Jesus,
We're so glad that You've redeemed us, precious Jesus;
And we lift our hands before You
As a token of our love,
Precious Jesus, precious Jesus,

Holy Spirit, Holy Spirit,
Come and fill our hearts anew, Holy Spirit.
And we lift our voice before You
As a token of our love,
Holy Spirit, Holy Spirit.

Hallelujah, hallelujah,
Hallelujah, hallelujah –
And we lift our hearts before You
As a token of our love,
Hallelujah, hallelujah.

773

Bryn Haworth.

HOLY, HOLY, HOLY IS THE LORD.
Holy, holy, holy is the Lord.

And He is precious in God's sight,
So precious in His eyes.

Worthy, worthy, worthy is the Lamb.
Worthy, worthy, worthy is the Lamb.

Glory, I give glory to the Lamb of God.
Glory, I give glory to the Lamb of God.

774 Richard Lewis.

HOLY, HOLY, LORD GOD ALMIGHTY,
Who was and who is
And is to come.
(Repeat)

All the angels cry 'holy,'
All the angels cry 'holy,'
All the angels cry 'holy is Your name.
Holy is Your name.
Holy is Your name.
Holy is Your name.
Holy is Your name.'

775 John Paculabo.

HOLY IS YOUR NAME,
Yeshua, my Deliverer.
Worthy of all praise,
You everliving God.

Perfect are Your ways,
Jehovah, my Father.
Faithful is Your love,
You gave Yourself for me.

In You I have security;
In You I put my trust.
In You I have confidence,
You meet my every need.

776

Mick Gisbey.

HOLY ONE, my life is in Your hand;
My song an offering of my heart,
Redeemed, washed clean,
By faith I stand secure.
In You, Jesus, I live.

To You the glory, to You the power,
To You the honour forever more.
Your love brings healing,
Your love's eternal,
Your love's the answer,
The hope of the world,
The hope of the world.

777

Charlotte Exon.

HOLY SPIRIT, MOVE WITHIN ME,
Holy Spirit, come upon me now.
Holy Spirit, lead me to
The secret place of prayer,
Manifest the glory of God.
Holy Spirit, You are welcome,
Holy Spirit, we desire You.
Holy Spirit, worship through us,
Let us see the glory of God.

778

Robert Newey.

HOPE OF THE WORLD,
You stepped into our time,
And yet they spurned You and then turned away.
To a dying world You reached out,
But they didn't want to hear
The words You had to say.

But may the light
You came to bring now shine
In a world that finally lost its way.
Holy love, now come,
Come flow though me,
Be my theme until my dying day.

Mercy, love, truth,
You shared all these
And then to bring them life
Became a dying seed.
Now to all who will receive
A new way has been opened,
And Your children are the light they need.

And may the light...

779

Graham Kendrick & Steve Thompson.

HOW CAN I BE FREE FROM SIN?
Lead me to the cross of Jesus.
From the guilt, the power, the pain?
Lead me to the cross of Jesus.
There's no other way,
No price that I could pay;
Simply to the cross I cling.
This is all I need,
This is all I plead,
That His blood was shed for me.

How can I know peace within?
Lead me to the cross of Jesus.
Sing a song of joy again!
Lead me to the cross of Jesus.
Flowing from above,
All-forgiving love
From the Father's heart to me!
What a gift of grace –
His own righteousness
Clothing me in purity!

How can I live day by day?
Lead me to the cross of Jesus.
Following His narrow way?
Lead me to the cross of Jesus.

780

Stuart Townend.

HOW DEEP THE FATHER'S LOVE FOR US,
How vast beyond all measure,
That He should give His only Son
To make a wretch His treasure.
How great the pain of searing loss –
The Father turns His face away,
As wounds which mar the Chosen One
Bring many sons to glory.

Behold the man upon a cross,
My sin upon His shoulders;
Ashamed, I hear my mocking voice
Call out among the scoffers.
It was my sin that held Him there
Until it was accomplished;
His dying breath has brought me life –
I know that it is finished.

I will not boast in anything,
No gifts, no power, no wisdom;
But I will boast in Jesus Christ,
His death and resurrection.
Why should I gain from His reward?
I cannot give an answer;
But this I know with all my heart –
His wounds have paid my ransom.

781

Matt Redman.

HOW LOVELY IS YOUR DWELLING PLACE,
O Lord Almighty.
My soul longs and even faints for You.
For here my heart is satisfied,
Within Your presence.
I sing beneath the shadow of Your wings.

Better is one day in Your courts,
Better is one day in Your house,
Better is one day in Your courts
Than thousands elsewhere.
(Repeat)

One thing I ask and I would seek;
To see Your beauty,
To find You in the place Your glory dwells.

My heart and flesh cry out
For You, the living God;
Your Spirit's water for my soul.
I've tasted and I've seen,
Come once again to me;
I will draw near to You,
I will draw near to You.

782

John Newton.

HOW SWEET THE NAME OF JESUS SOUNDS
In a believer's ear;
It soothes his sorrows, heals his wounds,
And drives away his fear.
It makes the wounded spirit whole,
And calms the troubled breast;
'Tis manna to the hungry soul
And to the weary, rest,
And to the weary, rest.

Dear name, the Rock on which I build,
My shield, and hiding place;
My never failing treasury, filled
With boundless stores of grace.
Jesus, my Shepherd, Saviour, Friend,
My Prophet, Priest, and King;
My Lord, my Life, my Way, my End,
Accept the praise I bring,
Accept the praise I bring.

Weak is the effort of my heart,
And cold my warmest thought;
But when I see You as You are,
I'll praise You as I ought.
I would Your boundless love proclaim
With every fleeting breath;
So shall the music of Your name
Refresh my soul in death,
Refresh my soul in death.

783

Dave Bilbrough.

HOW WONDERFUL, *how glorious*
Is the love of God,
Bringing healing, forgiveness,
Wonderful love.

Let celebration echo through this land;
We bring reconciliation,
We bring hope to every man:

We proclaim the kingdom
Of our God is here;
Come and join the heavenly anthem,
Ringing loud and ringing clear:

Listen to the music
As His praises fill the air;
With joy and with gladness
Tell the people everywhere:

784

Dave Bilbrough.

HUMBLE YOURSELVES
Under God's mighty hand,
So that He will lift you up.
(Repeat)

Cast all anxiety
On Him,
Because He cares for You.

Open your hearts
To the Lord your God,
And know His love for you.
(Repeat)

Cast all anxiety
On Him,
Because He cares for You.

I bow down
Before You, my Lord.
(Repeat)

785 Jim Bailey.

I AM THE APPLE OF GOD'S EYE,
His BANANA over me is love.
He ORANGES His angels to look after me,
As His blessings PLUM-met from above.

Never have to play the GOOSEBERRY,
Feel like a LEMON, no not me.
For wherever this MAN-GOES,
A RASPBERRY it never blows.

The GREAT FRUIT of God,
The GREAT FRUIT of God,
The GREAT FRUIT of God it overflows.
(Repeat)

I will praise Him on the TANGERINE,
Praise Him on the MANDARIN;
SATSUMA or later you will see
There is always a CLEMENTINE for praising Him.

786 David Gate.

I AM YOURS
And You are mine,
Friend to me
For all of time.

And all I have now
I give to You.
And all I want now
Is to be pure, pure like You.

I'm not afraid
Of earthly things,
For I am safe
With You, my King.

787

Wayne Drain.

I BELIEVE IN GOD THE FATHER,
I believe in Jesus the Son:
I believe in God the Holy Spirit,
I believe in the Three in One.

I believe He was born of a virgin,
Was crucified and buried in the ground.
Descended into hell and won the battle,
But the devil, death and hell
Couldn't hold Him down.

O Lord, we're drowning in confusion,
So many of us going separate ways;
Wanting to be God is our delusion,
But some of us are standing up,
Not ashamed to say, I believe, I believe!

I believe He ascended into heaven,
Where He sits at God's right hand;
And I believe our King will be returning
To judge the living and the dead,
From every tribe and land.

788

Dave Bilbrough.

I BELIEVE THERE IS A GOD IN HEAVEN
Who paid the price for all my sin;
Shed His blood to open up the way
For me to walk with Him.

Gave His life upon a cross,
Took the punishment for us,
Offered up Himself in love,
Jesus, Jesus.

'It is finished' was His cry;
Not even death could now deny
The Son of God exalted high,
Jesus, Jesus,
Jesus.

789

David Fellingham.

I BOW DOWN in humble adoration,
Speak Your name with love and devotion,
Jesus, the Lamb sacrificed for me.
I see Your face, Your tender hands
Scarred for me.
I fall at Your feet with songs of praises singing;
My joy is complete, You fulfil my longing.
Prophet of God, my Priest and my King,
I worship and adore.

Before the Father's throne You ever intercede;
You always hear my prayer, whatever I may plead.
You wipe away my tears, You give me victory;
By Your blood I am cleansed, I am free.

790

Martin Smith.

(Oh) **I COULD SING UNENDING SONGS**
Of how You saved my soul.
Well, I could dance a thousand miles
Because of Your great love.

My heart is bursting, Lord,
To tell of all You've done,
Of how You changed my life
And wiped away the past.
I wanna shout it out,

From every rooftop sing,
For now I know that God is for me,
Not against me.

Everybody's singing now,
'Cause we're so happy!
Everybody's dancing now,
'Cause we're so happy!
If only we could see Your face,
And see You smiling over us,
And unseen angels celebrate,
For joy is in this place!

791

Craig Musseau.

I CRY OUT
For your hand of mercy to heal me.
I am weak,
I need Your love to free me.
O Lord, my Rock,
My strength in weakness,
Come rescue me, O Lord.

You are my hope,
Your promise never fails me.
And my desire
Is to follow You forever.
For You are good,
For You are good,
For You are good to me.
For You are good,
For You are good,
For You are good to me.

792

Ian Smale.

I DON'T WANT TO BE A PHARISEE
Or anyone like that.
It's stupid swallowing camels
Whilst straining out a gnat.
To keep the letter of the law,
They forgot the people it was for.
So I don't want to be a Pharisee,
I don't want to be a Pharisee,
I don't want to be a Pharisee
Or anyone like that.

793

Matt Redman.

I DREAM of tongues of fire
Resting on Your people,
I dream of all the miracles to come.
I hope to see the coming
Healing of the nations,
I long to see the prodigals return.
So many hopes and longings in You;
When will all the dreams come true?

I'm a believer in Your kingdom,
I am a seeker of the new things,
I am a dreamer with some old dreams,
Let them now come.

I hope to see You come down,
Rend the mighty heavens,
And let Your glory cover all the earth;
To see Your sons and daughters
Come to know and love You,
And find a purer passion in the church.
These are the things my heart will pursue:
When will all the dreams come true?

May Your church now reach out,
Sowing truth and justice,
Learn to love the poor and help the weak.
When Your kingdom's coming
It will touch the broken,
Place the lonely in a family.
So many hopes and longings in You:
When will all the dreams come true?

794

Graham Kendrick.

IF MY PEOPLE, who bear My name,
Will humble themselves and pray;
If they seek My presence
And turn their backs on their wicked ways:
Then I will hear from heaven,
I'll hear from heaven and will forgive;
I will forgive their sins
And will heal their land,
Yes, I will heal their land.

795

Tommy Walker.

I HAVE A MAKER,
He formed my heart;
Before even time began
My life was in His hand.

I have a Father,
He calls me His own;
He'll never leave me,
No matter where I go.

He knows my name,
He knows my every thought;
He sees each tear that falls,
And hears me when I call.

796

Matt Redman.

I HAVE COME TO LOVE YOU,
I have come to love You today.
(Repeat)

And today and forever more
I'll love Your name.
And today and forever more
I'll love Your name.

I have come to worship,
I have come to worship today.
(Repeat)

I have come to thank You,
I have come to thank You today.
(Repeat)

797

Stuart Townend.

I HAVE HEARD that You are swift to bless the seeker,
And I believe that You will hear the constant cry;
So I will call until I know I've had an answer,
I need Your power, Lord!
As Jacob wrestled, so I'll wrestle with Your angel,
And though I'm weary, I will not be overcome;
For You have given me a passion for Your kingdom,
O let Your glory fall!

I won't let go,
I won't let go until You bless me.
I won't take no for an answer;
Jesus, I won't let go!

I have heard that You show mercy to a nation,
And I believe that You give power to Your church;
So now I'm asking You to open up the heavens,
Pour out Your mercy, Lord!
For Your gospel to be lived among Your people,
For Your miracle of healing on the streets;
For the government to fear the Lord Almighty,
We need Your power, Lord!

I'm not ungrateful for the blessings You have given,
But I can see the need around me;
I'm not ashamed to say I need all that You have,
So Father, hear me knocking,
See me holding out my hands to You.

For a hunger that will overcome my weakness,
For a love that will not seek its own reward;
For my life to make a difference in this nation,
I need Your power, Lord!

798

Kent Henry.

(And) **I HAVE LOVED YOU** *with an everlasting love,*
And I have drawn you with My loving kindness.
And I have loved you with an everlasting love,
And I have drawn you with My loving kindness.

Because God loved you and to keep His own,
He brought you out with a mighty hand,
He redeemed you from the devil's yoke.
Oh, the Lord, He is the God
And faithful is He.
He'll keep His word and His covenant,
Giving mercy and prosperity.

And casting all of Your cares on Him
For He cares for you,
There's a love dimension
In the kingdom of God,
It's sure to take you through.
God commanded His love toward us,
Christ died on a tree,
Then He rose again, the living God,
More than conquerors now are we.

799

Lynn DeShazo.

I HAVE MADE YOU TOO SMALL IN MY EYES;
O Lord, forgive me.
And I have believed in a lie
That You were unable to heal me.
But now, O Lord, I see my wrong;
Heal my heart, and show Yourself strong.
And in my eyes and with my song,
O Lord, be magnified,
O Lord, be magnified.

Be magnified, O Lord;
You are highly exalted.
And there is nothing You can't do,
O Lord, my eyes are on You,
Be magnified,
O Lord, be magnified.

I have leaned on the wisdom of men;
O God, forgive me.
And I have responded to them
Instead of Your light and Your mercy.
But now, O Lord, I see my wrong;
Heal my heart and show Yourself strong.
And in my eyes and with my song,
O Lord, be magnified,
O Lord, be magnified.

800

Don Moen.

I JUST WANT TO BE WHERE YOU ARE,
Dwelling daily in Your presence.
I don't want to worship from afar,
Draw me near to where You are.
I just want to be where You are,
In Your dwelling place forever.
Take me to the place where You are,
I just want to be with You.

I want to be where You are,
Dwelling in You presence,
Feasting at Your table,
Surrounded by Your glory.
In Your presence,
That's where I always want to be,
I just want to be,
I just want to be with You.

O my God, You are my strength and my song,
And when I'm in Your presence,
Though I'm weak, You're always strong.

801

Nathan Fellingham.

I KNOW A PLACE
Where blessings from heaven are poured,
Mercy and grace abounding.
Through Jesus' blood
We have now been set free
Into the Father's loving.

I know a place
Where there is no guilt or fear,
As I come into His presence.
I can now know
A peace which surpasses all,
Nothing shall separate us.

And I will trust in You alone,
My refuge and strength.
For all the trials that come my way,
Your grace is sufficient for me.

I know a place
Where a wonderful river flows,
That fills me with His glory;
Bringing us life,
We're stirred to adore Him,
A perfect joy everlasting.

802

Randy & Terry Butler.

I KNOW A PLACE, A WONDERFUL PLACE,
Where accused and condemned
Find mercy and grace.
Where the wrongs we have done,
And the wrongs done to us
Were nailed there with Him (You)
There on the cross.

(Men) At the cross,
(Women) At the cross,
(All) He (You) died for my sin.
(Men) At the cross,
(Women) At the cross,
(All) He (You) gave us life again.

803

Matt Redman.

I KNOW YOU LOVE TO CROWN THE HUMBLE,
Pouring out grace for the broken heart.
You bless the meek, You meet the lowly;
Lord, as I bow, lift me to You.

I keep on bowing down, bowing down,
Keep on bowing down,
What else can I do?
Keep on bowing down, bowing down.
What else can I do,
To give it all to You?

I'd like to be one such believer,
Keeping my knees firmly on the ground.
I'd like to tread humbly before You;
Lord, as I bow, lift me to You.

Do You smile when You see
A humble believer on their knees?
And my Lord, will You be pleased
To look upon me, to look upon me?

804

Timothy Dudley-Smith.

I LIFT MY EYES TO THE QUIET HILLS,
In the press of a busy day;
As green hills stand in a dusty land,
So God is my strength and stay.

I lift my eyes to the quiet hills,
To a calm that is mine to share;
Secure and still in the Father's will,
And kept by the Father's care.

I lift my eyes to the quiet hills,
With a prayer as I turn to sleep;
By day, by night,
Through the dark and light,
My Shepherd will guard His sheep.

I lift my eyes to the quiet hills,
And my heart to the Father's throne;
In all my ways to the end of days,
The Lord will preserve His own.

805

Steve & Vikki Cook.

I LONG FOR YOU, O LORD.
I long to know You more;
I long to have Your heart placed in me every day.
I long for, I long for You, O Lord.

I hunger to eat the bread
Only You can give.
I'm thirsting to drink Your water
That I might live,
To grow in You,
To know in You
My every desire is found.

806

Ian White.

I LOVE THE LORD for He has heard me,
He has heard my mercy plea.
From deep within my troubled heart,
I cried 'O Lord, save me!'
I love the Lord for His compassion
And His gracious, righteous ways.
He protects the simple-hearted ones,
And in my need,
The Lord saw me, and saved.

For as long, for as long as I live,
I will call, I will call on His name.
Be at rest once more, my soul,
For the Lord is good,
And He has been good to you.

I love the Lord for all the goodness
That I never can repay,
But I lift the cup of salvation,
And call upon His name.
I will fulfil my vows before the Lord,
In the presence of His saints;
O, make me now Your servant, Lord,
You have freed me from,
You have freed me from these chains.

807

Phil Lawson Johnston.

I LOVE YOU, LORD, MY STRENGTH,
For You heard my cry.
You have been my help in trouble.
I've put my trust in You,
My refuge and my hope,
You're the Rock on which I stand.

You're my stronghold,
You're my stronghold,
You're the stronghold of my life.
You're my stronghold,
You're my stronghold,
You're the stronghold of my life.

I love You, Lord, my strength,
You reached down from on high,
And You rescued me from trouble.
You've taken hold of me,
And set me on a rock,
And now this is where I stand.

I love You, Lord, my strength,
There is no other rock,
And now I will not be shaken.
The sea may roar and crash,
The mountains quake and fall,
Ah, but on this Rock I stand.

808

Doug Horley.

I'M A FRIEND OF JESUS CHRIST, *(echo)*
He's God's Son and He's alive, *(echo)*
I will trust in Him it's true, *(echo)*
He's always there to see me through.*(echo)*

Sound off, *Jesus!*
Sound off, is *Lord!*
Sound off, *Jesus!*
Sound off, is *Lord!*

The gift of God is eternal life through Jesus Christ,
(Repeat x3)
Through Jesus, Jesus Christ.

Jesus is the Boss of my life,
He's the only one can make it come right.
Jesus is the Boss of my life,
Jesus is the Boss.

(Rap)
I said, come on everybody and move your feet;
The rhythm is hot, it's a powerful beat.
The time is right to do some business,
Get on your feet and be a witness
To the Holy One,
The King of kings, God's only Son;
Jesus Christ, that's His name,
He died to take our sin and shame.

809

Ian Smale.

I'M LOOKING UP TO JESUS,
His face is shining beauty.
I'm feeling so unworthy,
Yet His Spirit leads me on.
I'm looking up to Jesus,
His radiance surrounds me.
I feel so pure and clean,
A taste of heaven on earth.

(Last time)
I'm looking up to Jesus.

810

Kevin Prosch.

I'M STANDING HERE TO TESTIFY, *(Leader)*
O, the Lord is good. *(All)*
To sing of how He changed my heart. *(Leader)*
O, the Lord is good. *(All)*
I was bound by hate and pride, *(Leader)*
O, the Lord is good. *(All)*
Never knowing of His light. *(Leader)*
O, the Lord is good. *(All)*

I did not think I could have peace, *(Leader)*
O, the Lord is good. *(All)*
Trapped inside by fear and shame. *(Leader)*
O, the Lord is good. *(All)*
He wiped away all of my grief, *(Leader)*
O, the Lord is good. *(All)*
When I believed upon His name. *(Leader)*

Come to the light, come as you are;
You can be the friend of God.
Humble yourself, give Him your heart,
He will meet you where you are.

(Last chorus)
Come to the light, just as you are;
Fall on the Rock for the wasted years.
He will restore all that was lost,
Surrender now, His power is here.

Clap Your hands, O God.
Clap Your hands, O God.
(Repeat)

811

Chris Bowater.

I NEED YOU like dew in the desert,
Like refreshing summer rain,
Come and pour Your love again on me.
I'm finding that every time I come
And ask for something more,
You never fail to pour Your love on me.

And peace like a river flows,
Waves of mercy ever roll;
Take me deeper,
I want to know You more.
Pour Your love, pour Your love,
Pour Your love on me.

812

David Fellingham.

IN EVERY CIRCUMSTANCE of life
You are with me, glorious Father.
And I have put my trust in You,
That I may know the glorious hope
To which I'm called.
And by the power that works in me,
You've raised me up and set me free;
And now in every circumstance

I'll prove Your love without a doubt,
Your joy shall be my strength,
Your joy shall be my strength.

813

Jacques Berthier/Taizé.

IN GOD ALONE my soul can find rest and peace,
In God my peace and joy.
Only in God my soul can find its rest,
Find its rest and peace.

Mon âme se repose en paix sur Dieu seul:
De lui vient mon salut.
Oui, sur Dieu seul mon âme se repose,
Se repose en paix.

814

Geoff Bullock.

IN MY LIFE PROCLAIM YOUR GLORY,
In my heart reveal Your majesty;
Then my soul shall speak the wonders of Your grace,
And this heart of mine shall sing Your praise.
In my words proclaim Your mercy,
In my life reveal Your power;
Then my soul shall be a mirror of Your love,
And this heart of mine shall sing Your praise.

Lord of all mercy, God of all grace,
Lord of all righteousness;
Lord of the heavens, Lord of the earth
Enthroned in majesty.
Worthy of honour, worthy of praise,
All glory and majesty;
I give You the honour, I give You the praise,
And proclaim Your glorious power.

In my soul unveil Your love, Lord,
Deep within my heart renewing me.
Day by day your life transforming all I am,
As this heart of mine reflects Your praise.
Lord of all, enthroned in glory,
Grace and mercy, truth and righteousness,
Every knee shall bow before this Christ, our Lord,
As all creation sings Your praise.

815

John Pantry.

IN MYSTERY REIGNING, King over all,
Hear angels proclaiming, Jesus is Lord.
To each generation Your love is the same;
Wonderful Saviour, we worship Your name.

A beauty that's timeless, who can compare?
All earth stands in silence, when You appear.
Your kingdom is boundless, Your love without end;
Wonder of wonders, this King is my friend!

All power has been given into Your hands;
Through blood and by suffering You now command.
And no opposition can stand in Your light;
Crowned King of heaven, we kneel at the sight.

816

Wayne Drain.

IN MY WEAKNESS You are strong,
When I fall short You carry me along.
Into my darkness You shine Your light,
When I feel blinded, You restore my sight.

You are the Lord, You never change,
You still the storm when I call Your name.
You're all I want, You're always there,
No matter when, no matter where.
You're the Lord, You never change.
You're the Lord, You never change.

I'm inconsistent, but You are true;
I don't trust myself, but I depend on You.
Look through my selfishness, and see my heart;
Bring out the precious from the worthless parts.

I need courage, Lord, to make a change;
It's time my independence got rearranged.
I'm tired of chasing after my own ways;
So I'll serve You, Lord,
Serve You, Lord, serve You, Lord,
For the rest, rest of my days.

817

Jacques Berthier/Taizé.

IN THE LORD I'll be ever thankful,
In the Lord I will rejoice!
Look to God, do not be afraid;
Lift up your voices, the Lord is near,
Lift up your voices, the Lord is near.

El Senyor és la meva força,
El Senyor el meu cant.
Ell m'haestat la salvació
En ell confio, i no tinc por.
En ell confio, i no tinc por.

818

Author unknown.

IN THE NAME OF JESUS,
In the name of Jesus,
We have the victory.

In the name of Jesus,
In the name of Jesus,
Demons will have to flee.
Who can tell what God can do?
Who can tell of His love for you?
In the name of Jesus, Jesus,
We have the victory.

819

Sue Rinaldi & Steve Bassett.

IN THESE DAYS OF DARKNESS,
Who will bear the light?
In all of this confusion,
Who will rage against the night?
And who will light a beacon
In the face of this dark, dark sky?

Where there is oppression,
Who will raise the flame?
For the sake of all the children,
Who will touch the fields of shame?
And who will light a beacon
In the face of this dark, dark sky,
With a hope that is eternal,
With a love that will never die?

Oh I, I will carry the fire.
Oh I, I will carry the fire.

Who will burn with passion,
Blazing from the heart,
To forge a new tomorrow?
We must tell the world
Of a hope that is eternal,
Of a love that will never die.
And we will light a beacon
In the face of this dark, dark sky.

Oh I, I will carry the fire.
Oh I, I will carry the fire.
I will not rest, I will not tire,
With all my strength I'll carry the fire.
I will not rest, I will not tire,
With all my strength I'll carry the fire.

820

David Fellingham.

IN THESE DAYS OF REFRESHING,
In these days of visitation,
There is a reason why You've come.
We have tasted of Your fulness,
One blessing after another,
And that is the reason we say 'come'.

It's not just to make us laugh or cry,
To shake or fall, but to glorify
Jesus, Jesus, Jesus,
And that is the reason we say 'come'.

And let me know the power to speak
And witness for the gospel,
Let me know the power to pray for the sick
And see them healed.
Let me know the faith that can
Move the mighty mountain,
Let me know the love that joins me
To Your people.

And we say more, Lord,
More of Your power.
We say more, Lord,
More of Your power.
We say more, Lord,
More of Your power,
More of Your power in me.

821

Maggi Dawn.

INTO THE DARKNESS of this world,
Into the shadows of the night;
Into this loveless place You came,
Lightened our burdens, eased our pain,
And made these hearts Your home.
Into the darkness once again –
Oh come, Lord Jesus, come.

Come with Your love
To make us whole,
Come with Your light
To lead us on,
Driving the darkness
Far from our souls:
O come, Lord Jesus, come.

Into the longing of our souls,
Into these heavy hearts of stone,
Shine on us now Your piercing light,
Order our lives and souls aright,
By grace and love unknown,
Until in You our hearts unite –
Oh come, Lord Jesus, come.

O Holy Child, Emmanuel,
Hope of the ages, God with us,
Visit again this broken place,
Till all the earth declares Your praise
And Your great mercies own.
Now let Your love be born in us,
O come, Lord Jesus, come.

(Last Chorus)
Come in Your glory,
Take Your place,
Jesus, the Name above all names,
We long to see You face to face,
O come, Lord Jesus, come.

822

Ian Smale.

I ONCE WAS FRIGHTENED OF SPIDERS,
I once was frightened of the dark;
I once was frightened of many, many things,
Especially things that barked.
But now I'm asking Jesus
To help these fears to go,
'Cause I don't want them to be part of me,
No, no, no, no, no.

I once was frightened by thunder,
And frightened by lightning too;
I once was frightened by many, many things
That crashed and banged and blew.
But now I'm asking Jesus
To help these fears to go,
'Cause I don't want them to be part of me,
No, no, no, no, no.

823

Graham Kendrick.

IS ANYONE THIRSTY, anyone?
Is anyone thirsty?
Is anyone thirsty, anyone?
Is anyone thirsty? Jesus said:
'Let them come to me and drink,
Let them come to me.'

O, let the living waters flow,
O, let the living waters flow,
Let the river of Your Spirit
Flow through me.
(Repeat)
Flow through me.

Let the living waters flow.
Let the living waters flow.
Let the living waters flow.
Let the living waters flow.

824

Chris Falson.

I SEE THE LORD
Seated on the throne, exalted:
And the train of His robe
Fills the temple with glory:
The whole earth is filled,
The whole earth is filled,
The whole earth is filled
With Your glory.

Holy, holy,
Holy, holy,
Yes, holy is the Lord.
Holy, holy,
Holy, holy,
Yes, holy is the Lord of lords.

825

Craig Musseau.

I SING A SIMPLE SONG OF LOVE
To my Saviour, to my Jesus.
I'm grateful for the things You've done,
My loving Saviour, oh precious Jesus.
My heart is glad that You've called me Your own;
There's no place I'd rather be,

(Than) in Your arms of love,
In Your arms of love,
Holding me still,
Holding me near
In Your arms of love.

826

Terry MacAlmon.

I SING PRAISES TO YOUR NAME, O Lord,
Praises to Your name, O Lord,
For Your name is great and greatly to be praised.
I sing praises to Your name, O Lord,
Praises to Your name, O Lord,
For Your name is great and greatly to be praised.

I give glory to Your name...

827

Martin Smith.

IS IT TRUE TODAY that when people pray,
Cloudless skies will break,
Kings and queens will shake?
Yes it's true, and I believe it,
I'm living for You.

Well it's true today that when people pray
We'll see dead men rise,
And the blind set free.
Yes it's true and I believe it,
I'm living for You.

I'm gonna be a history maker in this land.
I'm gonna be a speaker of truth
To all mankind.
I'm gonna stand,
I'm gonna run into Your arms,
Into Your arms again,
Into Your arms, into Your arms again.

Well it's true today that when people stand
With the fire of God and the truth in hand,
We'll see miracles, we'll see angels sing,

We'll see broken hearts making history.
Yes it's true, and I believe it,
I'm living for You.

828

Paul Oakley.

I STAND AMAZED when I realise
Your love for me is beyond all measure.
Lord, I can't deny
Your love for me is great.

It's as high, high as the heavens above,
Such is the depth of Your love
Toward those who fear You.
O Lord, far as the east is from west,
You have removed my transgressions.
You make my life brand new:
Father, I love You.

Your love is higher,
High as the heavens.
Your love is deeper,
Deeper than the deepest ocean.
Your love is stronger,
Stronger than the powers of darkness.
Your love is sweeter,
Sweeter than wine.

829

Charles Gabriel.

I STAND AMAZED IN THE PRESENCE
Of Jesus the Nazarene,
And wonder how He could love me,
A sinner, condemned, unclean.

How marvellous! How wonderful!
And my song shall ever be:
How marvellous! How wonderful!
Is my Saviour's love for me!

For me it was in the garden He prayed,
'Not My will, but Thine':
He had no tears for His own griefs,
But sweat drops of blood for mine.

In pity angels beheld Him,
And came from the world of light
To comfort Him in the sorrows
He bore for my soul that night.

He took my sins and my sorrows,
He made them His very own;
He bore the burden of Calvary,
And suffered and died alone.

When with the ransomed in glory
His face I at last shall see,
'Twill be my joy through the ages
To sing of His love for me.

830

Daniel L. Schutte.

I, THE LORD OF SEA AND SKY,
I have heard My people cry;
All who dwell in dark and sin
My hand will save.
I, who made the stars of night,
I will make their darkness bright.
I will speak My word to them.
Whom shall I send?

Here I am, Lord.
Is it I, Lord?
I have heard You calling in the night.
I will go, Lord,
If You lead me;
I will hold Your people in my heart.

I, the Lord of snow and rain,
I have borne my people's pain;
I have wept for love of them –
They turn away.
I will break their hearts of stone,
Give them hearts for love alone;
I will speak My word to them.
Whom shall I send?

I, the Lord of wind and flame,
I will tend the poor and lame,
I will set a feast for them –
My hand will save.
Finest bread I will provide
Till their hearts are satisfied;
I will give My life to them.
Whom shall I send?

831

John L. Bell & Graham Maule.

IT IS GOOD TO GIVE THANKS TO THE LORD,
To remember all He has done;
Then God will remember our praises
When He looks with love on His people.

O give thanks to the Lord,
For His love endures forever.
O give thanks to the Lord,
For the Lord alone is good.

Our sin is the sin of our fathers,
We have done wrong, we all have been evil;
Like those who once lived in bondage,
We paid no heed to all You had done.

Our fathers forsook Your love,
At the Red Sea they questioned their God;
They fell from their faith in the desert,
And put God to the test in the wilderness.

Time after time He would rescue them,
Yet in malice they dared to defy Him;
Despite this He came to their aid
When He heard their cries of distress.

Save us, O Lord, in Your love;
Bring us back from all that offends You.
Look not alone at our sins,
But remember Your promise of mercy.

Blessed be the Lord God of Israel
Both now and through all eternity;
Let nations and people cry out
And sing Amen! Alleluia!

832

Terry Butler.

IT IS THE CRY OF MY HEART *to follow You.*
It is the cry of my heart to be close to You.
It is the cry of my heart to follow
All of the days of my life.

Teach me Your holy ways, O Lord,
So I can walk in Your truth.
Teach me Your holy ways, O Lord,
And make me wholly devoted to You.

Open my eyes so I can see
The wonderful things that You do.
Open my heart up more and more
And make it wholly devoted to You.

833

Ian Smale.

**IT'S A WONDERFUL, WONDERFUL,
WONDERFUL FEELING,**
*It's a wonderful feeling to
Know you're saved.
It's a wonderful, wonderful,
Wonderful WONDERFUL!
Wonderful feeling to
Know you're saved.*

My life is built on rock, not sand;
It's a wonderful feeling to know you're saved.
And none can steal me from God's hand;
It's a wonderful feeling to know you're saved.

I once was lost but now I'm found:
It's a wonderful feeling to know you're saved.
In Father's arms I'm safe and sound:
It's a wonderful feeling to know you're saved.

My old life's gone, I'm now brand new:
It's a wonderful feeling to know you're saved.
Much less of me, much more of You:
It's a wonderful feeling to know you're saved.

834

Dave Bilbrough.

IT'S GETTING CLEARER, the light is dawning,
I'm pressing on to a higher place.
The past behind me, I'm moving forward,
And I will follow after You.

You are my strength, You are my shield,
You are the Rock on which I want to build my life,
O Lord, O Lord.
I won't compromise, I won't be denied,
I want to keep my eyes on the prize
Of knowing You, knowing You.

There is a passion that burns within me,
I long to see Your kingdom come.
To know Your presence, to seek no other;
I hunger, Lord, for more of You.

835

Matt Redman & Martin Smith.

IT'S RISING UP from coast to coast,
From north to south, and east to west;
The cry of hearts that love Your name,
Which with one voice we will proclaim.

The former things have taken place,
Can this be the new day of praise?
A heavenly song that comes to birth,
And reaches out to all the earth.
Oh, let the cry to nations ring,
That all may come and all may sing:

'Holy is the Lord.' (Every heart sing:)
'Holy is the Lord.' (With one voice sing:)
'Holy is the Lord.' (Every heart sing:)
'Holy is the Lord.'

And we have heard the Lion's roar,
That speaks of heaven's love and power.
Is this the time, is this the call
That ushers in Your kingdom rule?
Oh, let the cry to nations ring,
That all may come and all may sing:

'Jesus is alive!' (Every heart sing:)...

836

Pete Cant.

I'VE FALLEN IN LOVE (I've fallen in love)
Since the first time we met,
(Since the first time we met)
There at the cross where You paid for my sin,
You opened the way to my heart and came in,
Oh, I've fallen in love, (I've fallen in love)
Yes, I've fallen in love. (I've fallen in love)

I've fallen in love (I've fallen in love)
Since the first time we met,
(Since the first time we met)
When I finally looked unto You,
You broke my hardened heart in two,
Oh, I've fallen in love, (I've fallen in love)
Yes, I've fallen in love. (I've fallen in love.)

Jesus my Lord, only You have my heart,
Only You can know;
Words don't express what my heart tries to say,
That I have fallen in love.

I've fallen in love (I've fallen in love)
Since the first time we met,
(Since the first time we met)
When You stole my love of the world
And placed my heart's affection on You,
Oh, I've fallen in love, (I've fallen in love)
Yes, I've fallen in love. (I've fallen in love.)

837

Matt Redman.

I'VE GOT A LOVE SONG IN MY HEART,
It is for You, Lord my God.
I've got a love song in my heart,
It is for You, Lord my God.

La la la la la la la,
La la la la la la la,
La la la la la la la.
(Repeat)

I've got a passion in my heart...

I've got rejoicing in my heart...

And there is dancing in my heart...

I've never known a love like this...

838

Ian White.

I WAITED PATIENTLY for the Lord,
He turned and heard my cry.
He lifted me from the pit,
Out from the mud and mire.
He put my feet on a rock,
And gave me a firm place to stand.
He put a new song in my mouth,
A hymn of praise to God,
A hymn of praise to God.

Many will see, many will fear,
And many will put their trust in the Lord.
Many will see, many will fear,
And many will put their trust in the Lord.

Blessed is the man who trusts the Lord,
And turns from all the proud,
From all those who have turned aside,
To follow what is false.
Many are the wonders that You have done,
All the things You have planned;
Were I to count they still would be
Too many to declare,
Too many to declare.

839 Chris Falson.

I WALK BY FAITH,
Each step by faith,
To live by faith,
I put my trust in You.
(Repeat)

Every step I take is a step of faith;
No weapon formed against me shall prosper.
And every prayer I make is a prayer of faith;
And if my God is for me,
Then who can be against me?

840 Paul Oakley & Alan Rose.

I WANT TO BE HOLY,
I want to be righteous,
I want to live my life the way You want me to.
I want to be blameless,
Not walking in darkness,
I want to be a living sacrifice to You.

I'm gonna run the race,
I'm gonna run to win,
Throw off everything that hinders me.
I'm gonna fix my eyes upon the King,
And leave my sin behind.

I want to be so much better,
I want to be more like You.
Keep taking me further and deeper,
I want to right the wrong,
I want to live this song,
Now I'm pressing on,
I'm gonna leave my sin behind.

Singing, 'goodbye rage, goodbye hate,
Goodbye anger, goodbye malice,
Goodbye bitterness and slander,
Goodbye fear of man!'
(Repeat)

841

Doug Horley & Noel Richards.

I WANT TO BE OUT OF MY DEPTH IN YOUR LOVE,
Feeling Your arms so strong around me.
Out of my depth in Your love,
Out of my depth in You.
(Repeat)

Learning to let You lead,
Putting all trust in You;
Deeper into Your arms,
Surrounded by You.
Things I have held so tight,
Made my security;
Give me the strength I need
To simply let go.

842

Evan Rogers.

I WANT TO KNOW
The glorious inheritance
That You have given to me.
And I want to know
The hope that You have called me to,
O Lord, I want to know Your truth.

I want to know You better,
The Spirit without measure,
To know the fulness that's in You.

I want to know Your mystery,
The grace You've given freely,
I know my life is hidden in You.

I want to know
Your wisdom and Your revelation,
Drawing me to You.
I want to know
The power of Your mighty strength
Which raised
Jesus from the dead.

843

Paul Oakley.

I WAS LOST without a trace,
All except for the eyes of heaven.
Now my Saviour's love has found me,
And His love has brought me home.

I can sleep in peace tonight,
I won't worry about tomorrow,
Now I know my Daddy loves me,
And His perfect love will conquer all.

I'm like a child in His eyes,
And He will meet my needs
With all the riches of heaven;
And He loves me much too much
To let me go,
He will keep me in His love.

Heaven and earth may pass away,
And mountains fall into the ocean;
But His word is everlasting,
And His love goes on and on.

844

Brian Doerksen.

I WILL BE YOURS,
You will be mine
Together in eternity.
Our hearts of love
Will be entwined,
Together in eternity,
Forever in eternity.

No more tears of pain in our eyes;
No more fear or shame,
For we will be with You,
For we will be with You.

845

Martin J. Nystrom.

I WILL COME AND BOW DOWN
At Your feet, Lord Jesus.
In Your presence is fulness of joy.
There is nothing, there is no one
Who compares with You;
I take pleasure in worshipping You, Lord.

846

Steve Bassett & Sue Rinaldi.

I WILL CRY MERCY,
I will cry mercy for this land, O God.
I will cry justice,
I will cry justice for this land, O God,
For this land, O God.
Let Your tears flow from my eyes;
Let Your passion melt my heart of stone.
Let Your beauty be seen in my life;

Let Your heartbeat be my own.
So I'll cry mercy for this nation,
Let us see healing for the people,
And I'll cry justice for this nation, O God.

847

Matt Redman.

I WILL DANCE, I will sing,
To be mad for my King.
Nothing, Lord, is hindering
The passion in my soul.
(Repeat)

And I'll become
Even more undignified than this.
(Some would say it's foolishness but)
I'll become
Even more undignified than this.

Na, na, na, na, na, na! Hey!
Na, na, na, na, na, na! Hey!

848

Ian White.

I WILL EXTOL THE LORD with all my heart.
I will extol the Lord with all my heart,
For holy and awesome,
For holy and awesome,
For holy and awesome is His name.

Holy and awesome is His name.
Holy and awesome is His name.
And the fear of the Lord
Is the start of wisdom.
Holy and awesome is His name.

Holy and awesome is His name.
Holy and awesome is His name.
Those who follow His ways
Have a good understanding.
Holy and awesome is His name.

Holy and awesome is His name.
Holy and awesome is His name.
And to Him belong eternal praise.
Holy and awesome is His name.
Holy and awesome is His name.
Holy and awesome is His name.

849

Sue Rinaldi.

I WILL FOLLOW YOU TO THE CROSS
And lay myself down, lay myself down.
I will follow You to the cross,
And lay myself down, lay myself down.

Rid me of these dirty clothes,
Cleanse me from all this pollution.
I choose to walk in purity,
Oh, purify me, purify me.

Kiss me with Your healing touch,
Take me to the heat of the fire;
Bathe me in Your liquid love,
Oh, saturate me, saturate me.

Humbly I stand, humbly I kneel,
Humbly I fall at Your throne.
With a craving for You
That no words can describe:
Saturate me, saturate me;
Saturate me, saturate me;
Purify me, purify me;
Purify me, purify me;
Purify me, purify me.

850

Mark Altrogge.

I WILL GIVE THANKS TO THE LORD with all my heart,
I will sing glorious praises to Your name;
I will be glad and exalt in You, my Lord,
Yesterday, today, forever, You're the same.

O Most High,
You who are my stronghold,
When troubles come,
You're my hiding place;
O Most High,
Those who know You trust You,
You will not forsake the ones
Who seek Your face.

851

Matt Redman.

I WILL OFFER UP MY LIFE
In spirit and truth,
Pouring out the oil of love
As my worship to You.
In surrender I must give my every part;
Lord, receive the sacrifice
Of a broken heart.

Jesus, what can I give, what can I bring
To so faithful a friend, to so loving a King?
Saviour, what can be said, what can be sung
As a praise of Your name
For the things You have done?
Oh, my words could not tell, not even in part,
Of the debt of love that is owed by this thankful
heart.

You deserve my every breath
For You've paid the great cost;
Giving up Your life to death,
Even death on a cross.
You took all my shame away,
There defeated my sin,
Opened up the gates of heaven,
And have beckoned me in.

852

Bryn Haworth.

I WILL PRAISE YOU,
O Lord, with all of my heart.
I will praise You,
O Lord, with all of my heart.
Before the gods I will sing Your praise.
Before the gods I will praise Your name.

The Lord will fulfil His purpose for me.
The Lord will fulfil His purpose for me.
Do not forsake the work of Your hands,
Revive me, Lord.

You have exalted above all things
Your name and Your word.
You have exalted above all things
Your name and Your word.
I called to You, and You answered me.
When I called to You, You made me strong.

For Your love, O Lord, endures forever,
And Your faithfulness is to the clouds.
Do not forsake the work of Your hands,
Revive me, Lord.

853

Ian White.

I WILL PRAISE YOU WITH THE HARP
For Your faithfulness, O my God.
I will sing my praise to You
With the lyre, with the lyre.

O Holy One of Israel, (x3)
My lips will shout for joy,
My lips will shout for joy.

When I sing my praise to You, (x3)
For I have been redeemed,
I have been redeemed!

I'll speak of all Your righteous acts, (x3)
And tell them all day long,
And tell them all day long.

Those who want to harm me
Are put to shame and confused.
I will sing my praise to You
With the lyre, with the lyre.

I've been redeemed, I've been redeemed!
I've been redeemed, I've been redeemed!

854

Geoff Bullock.

I WILL REST IN CHRIST
Like the calm within the storm;
I can find security in Him who leads me on.
I will put my faith, my trust and every hope,
For the peace of God will touch my soul,
In Him I will be whole.

I am not dismayed, I am not cast down;
I will never be alone, I need never fear.
I can always hope, I can always love;
For the love of God has touched my heart,
In Him I am secure.

I will rest in Christ;
I will hope in Him.
I will find a place of comfort,
I can find a place of rest,
Held in love, loved in Him,
Safe, I am secure,
As I rest in Christ,
As I hope in Him.

I will trust in Christ
Like a rock in stormy seas;
I have found a shelter in His life and peace in me.
I have found the way,
The truth, this perfect life;
And the hope in me is found in Him,
The lover of my soul.

855

Max Dyer.

I WILL SING, I WILL SING a song unto the Lord, *(3 times)*
Alleluia, glory to the Lord.

Allelu, alleluia, glory to the Lord,
Allelu, alleluia, glory to the Lord,
Allelu, alleluia, glory to the Lord,
Alleluia, glory to the Lord.

We will come, we will come as one before the Lord,
(3 times)
Alleluia, glory to the Lord.

If the Son, if the Son shall make you free, *(3 times)*
You shall be free indeed.

They that sow in tears shall reap in joy, *(3 times)*
Alleluia, glory to the Lord!

Every knee shall bow and every tongue confess, *(3 times)*
That Jesus Christ is Lord.

In His name, in His name we have the victory, *(3 times)*
Alleluia, glory to the Lord.

856

Stuart Townend.

I WILL SING OF THE LAMB,
Of the price that was paid for me,
Purchased by God,
Giving all He could give!
Here now I stand
In the garments of righteousness;
Death has no hold, for in Jesus I live.

I will sing of His blood
That flows for my wretchedness,
Wounds that are bared,
That I may be healed;
Power and compassion,
The marks of His ministry:
May they be mine as I harvest His field.

Oh, I will sing of the Lamb.
Oh, I will sing of the Lamb.
My heart fills with wonder,
My mouth fills with praise!
Hallelujah, hallelujah.

Once I was blind,
Yet believed I saw everything,
Proud in my ways,
Yet a fool in my part;
Lost and alone
In the company of multitudes,
Life in my body, yet death in my heart.

Oh, I will sing of the Lamb.
Oh, I will sing of the Lamb.
Oh, why should the King
Save a sinner like me?
Hallelujah, hallelujah.

What shall I give
To the Man who gave everything,
Humbling Himself
Before all He had made?
Dare I withold
My own life from His sovereignty?
I shall give all for the sake of His name!

Oh, I will sing of the Lamb.
Oh, I will sing of the Lamb.
I'll sing of His love
For the rest of my days!
Hallelujah, hallelujah.

857

Maggi Dawn.

I WILL WAIT for Your peace to come to me.
I will wait for Your peace to come to me,
And I'll sing in the darkness,
And I'll wait without fear,
And I'll sing in the darkness,
And I'll wait without fear.

858

I WILL WAVE MY HANDS in praise and adoration,
I will wave my hands in praise and adoration,
I will wave my hands in praise and adoration,
Praise and adoration to the living God.

For He's given me hands that just love clapping:
One, two, one, two, three,
And He's given me a voice
That just loves shouting:
'Hallelujah!'
He's given me feet that just love dancing:
One, two, one, two, three,
And He's put me in a being
That has no trouble seeing
That whatever I am feeling
He is worthy to be praised.

859

I WILL WORSHIP (I will worship)
WITH ALL OF MY HEART. (with all of my heart)
I will praise You (I will praise You)
With all of my strength. (all my strength)
I will seek You (I will seek You)
All of my days. (all of my days)
I will follow (I will follow)
All of Your ways. (all Your ways)

I will give You all my worship,
I will give You all my praise.
You alone I long to worship,
You alone are worthy of my praise.

I will bow down, (I will bow down)
Hail You as King. (hail You as King)
I will serve You, (I will serve You)
Give You everything. (give You everything)
I will lift up (I will lift up)
My eyes to Your throne, (my eyes to Your throne)
I will trust You, (I will trust You)
I will trust You alone. (trust You alone)

860

Nathan Fellingham, Luke Fellingham
& Louise Hunt.

I WORSHIP YOU, ALMIGHTY KING, the Holy One,
For You alone have filled me with new life.
My greatest Friend, You've redeemed my soul;
You've won my heart with Your great love.

I have tasted of Your goodness
And I've heard of Your fame,
So we enter into Your presence
To praise Your holy name.

We lift our voice and sing,
There's an extravagant praise
That fills our hearts,
For You are Lord and King
And we bless Your name.
We dance for joy and bring
Our adoration to our faithful God,
To You our everything,
We bring extravagant praise.
Sing hallelujah, sing hallelujah.
Sing hallelujah, sing hallelujah.

You've called me, Lord, to live for You in holiness,
I've been made clean and chosen as Your son.
Through Jesus Christ You've made me whole,
My heart is filled with love for You.

861

Callie Gerbrandt.

I WORSHIP YOU, O LORD,
In spirit and truth;
I bow my face before Your throne,
I praise You, Lord.

I glorify Your name,
I magnify Your name;
And I exalt You Lord over all,
I praise You, Lord.

862

Evan Rogers.

I WOULD RATHER BE a doorkeeper in Your house,
Than have the many things this world could offer.
All that I have gained I now count as loss,
There's nothing that compares to knowing You.

In Your presence is where I want to be,
The place where You reveal Your grace and glory.
Your presence brings me to my knees,
I bow down and declare that You are holy.

I would rather have one day in Your courts, O Lord,
Than have a thousand days somewhere else.
You are my sun and shield,
No good thing will you withhold,
For blessed are the ones who trust in You.

863

Andy Thorpe.

JESUS, (Jesus)
Jesus, (Jesus)
It's the Name above all names.
(Repeat)

And at the name of Jesus
Every knee shall bow,
And every tongue confess He is Lord.

864

Chris Bowater.

JESUS, AT YOUR NAME we bow the knee.
Jesus, at Your name we bow the knee.
Jesus at Your name we bow the knee,
And acknowledge You as Lord.

You are Christ,
You are the Lord;
Through Your Spirit in our lives
We know who You are.

865

Matt Redman.

JESUS CHRIST, I think upon Your sacrifice,
You became nothing, poured out to death.
Many times I've wondered at Your gift of life,
And I'm in that place once again.
And I'm in that place once again.

And once again I look upon
The cross where You died,
I'm humbled by Your mercy
And I'm broken inside.
Once again I thank You,
Once again I pour out my life.

Now You are exalted to the highest place,
King of the heavens, where one day I'll bow.
But for now, I marvel at this saving grace,
And I'm full of praise once again.
I'm full of praise once again.

Thank You for the cross,
Thank You for the cross,
Thank You for the cross, my Friend.
(Repeat)

866

Steve Israel & Gerrit Gustafson.

JESUS CHRIST IS THE LORD OF ALL,
Lord of all the earth.
Jesus Christ is the Lord of all,
Lord of all the earth.
Jesus Christ is the Lord of all,
Lord of all the earth.
Jesus Christ is the Lord of all,
Lord of all the earth.

Only one God over the nations,
Only one Lord of all.
In no other name is there salvation,
Jesus is Lord of all.

Jesus Christ is Lord of all.
Jesus Christ is Lord of all.
Jesus Christ is Lord of all.
Jesus Christ is Lord of all.

867 Martin Lore.

JESUS, FORGIVE ME.
Jesus, free me.
Jesus, touch me.
Jesus, fill me.

I lift my head, lift my heart,
Lift my soul to You.
I give my life, give myself,
Give it all to You.

Jesus, teach me.
Jesus, lead me.
Jesus, guide me.
Jesus, use me.

868 Don Harris & Martin J Nystrom.

JESUS, I AM THIRSTY,
Won't You come and fill me?
Earthly things have left me dry,
Only You can satisfy,
All I want is more of You.

All I want is more of You,
All I want is more of You;
Nothing I desire, Lord,
But more of You.
(Repeat)
More of You.

869

Judith Butler & Paul Hemingway.

JESUS, I LOVE YOU,
I worship and adore You.
Jesus, I love You,
Lord, I glorify Your name.

You are mighty, O Lord,
The Ancient of Days.
Your love stands forever,
Unfailing Your ways.

You are reigning on high,
Exalted King.
Your throne is eternal,
You are Lord over all.

870

Phil Lawson Johnston.

JESUS IS THE NAME WE HONOUR;
Jesus is the name we praise.
Majestic Name above all other names,
The highest heaven and earth proclaim
That Jesus is our God.

We will glorify,
We will lift Him high,
We will give Him honour and praise.
We will glorify,
We will lift Him high,
We will give Him honour and praise.

Jesus is the name we worship;
Jesus is the name we trust.
He is the King above all other kings,
Let all creation stand and sing
That Jesus is our God.

Jesus is the Father's splendour;
Jesus is the Father's joy.
He will return to reign in majesty,
And every eye at last shall see
That Jesus is our God.

871

Bryn Haworth.

JESUS, JESUS,
Son of God, Son of man,
Friend of sinners, gift of God.
Jesus, Jesus,
Light of life, Lord of all,
Full of grace and truth.

You have come to us,
Your presence has filled this place.
We will draw near to You,
We come, Lord, to seek Your face.

Jesus, Jesus,
My heart aches, my soul waits,
For Your healing, Lord, I pray.
Jesus, Jesus,
Mighty God, holy Child,
Name above all names.

Jesus, Jesus,
Son of God, Son of Man,
My soul thirsts for You.

872

JESUS, LAMB OF GOD,
I stand redeemed,
Washed in Your blood.
And in the holy place I'll bow
To worship and adore.

Jesus, conquering King,
You died for me,
You bore my sins.
Your love has brought me to my knees
To worship and adore,
To worship and adore.

How I love You,
How I love You,
How I love You,
How I love You,
How I love You.

873

JESUS, LOVER OF MY SOUL,
All consuming fire is in Your gaze.
Jesus, I want You to know
I will follow You all my days.
For no one else in history is like You,
And history itself belongs to You.
Alpha and Omega, You have loved me,
And I will share eternity with You.

It's all about You, Jesus,
And all this is for You,
For Your glory and Your fame.
It's not about me,

As if You should do things my way;
You alone are God,
And I surrender to Your ways.

874

J. Ezzy, D. Grul, S. McPherson.

JESUS, LOVER OF MY SOUL,
Jesus, I will never let You go:
You've taken me from the miry clay,
You've set my feet upon the rock and now I know:

I love You, I need You,
Though my world will fall,
I'll never let You go;
My Saviour, my closest Friend,
I will worship You until the very end.

875

Jacques Berthier/Taizé.

JESUS, REMEMBER ME
When You come into Your kingdom.
Jesus, remember me
When You come into Your kingdom.

876

Graham Kendrick.

JESUS, RESTORE TO US AGAIN
The gospel of Your holy name,
That comes with power, not words alone,
Owned, signed and sealed from heaven's throne.
Spirit and word in one agreed;
The promise to the power wed.

The word is near, here in our mouths
And in our hearts, the word of faith;
Proclaim it on the Spirit's breath: Jesus!

Your word, O Lord, eternal stands,
Fixed and unchanging in the heavens;
The Word made flesh, to earth come down
To heal our world with nail-pierced hands.
Among us here You lived and breathed,
You are the Message we received.

Spirit of truth, lead us, we pray
Into all truth as we obey,
And as God's will we gladly choose,
Your ancient powers again will prove
Christ's teaching truly comes from God,
He is indeed the living Word.

Upon the heights of this great land
With Moses and Elijah stand.
Reveal Your glory once again,
Show us Your face, declare Your name.
Prophets and law, in You complete
Where promises and power meet.

Grant us in this decisive hour
To know the Scriptures and the power;
The knowledge in experience proved,
The power that moves and works by love.
May word and works join hands as one,
The word go forth, the Spirit come.

877

Tanya Riches.

JESUS, WHAT A BEAUTIFUL NAME.
Son of God, Son of Man,
Lamb that was slain.

Joy and peace, strength and hope,
Grace that blows all fear away.
Jesus, what a beautiful name.

Jesus, what a beautiful name.
Truth revealed, my future sealed,
Healed my pain.
Love and freedom, life and warmth,
Grace that blows all fear away.
Jesus, what a beautiful name.

Jesus, what a beautiful name.
Rescued my soul, my stronghold,
Lifts me from shame.
Forgiveness, security, power and love,
Grace that blows all fear away.
Jesus, what a beautiful name.

878

Chris Bowater.

JUST THE MENTION OF YOUR NAME
Causes me to fall before You,
Tears flow as I adore You,
At the mention of Your name,
Just the mention of Your name.

Just the mention of Your name
Reaffirms the love that holds me,
Speaks once more of love that knows me,
At the mention of Your name,
Just the mention of Your name.

Jesus, Jesus,
Jesus, Jesus.
At the mention of Your name,
I worship.

879 George Herbert.

LET ALL THE WORLD in every corner sing:
'My God and King!'
The heavens are not too high;
His praise may thither fly:
The earth is not too low;
His praises there may grow.
Let all the world in every corner sing:
'My God and King!'

Let all the world in every corner sing:
'My God and King!'
The Church with psalms must shout,
No door can keep them out:
But, above all, the heart
Must bear the longest part.
Let all the world in every corner sing:
'My God and King!'

880

Matt Redman.

LET EVERYTHING THAT,
Everything that,
Everything that has breath
Praise the Lord.
(Repeat)

Praise You in the morning,
Praise You in the evening,
Praise You when I'm young
And when I'm old.
Praise You when I'm laughing,
Praise You when I'm grieving,
Praise You every season of the soul.

If we could see how much You're worth,
Your power, Your might, Your endless love,
Then surely we would never cease to praise :

Praise You in the heavens,
Joining with the angels,
Praising You forever and a day.
Praise You on the earth now,
Joining with creation,
Calling all the nations to Your praise.

If they could see how much You're worth,
Your power, Your might, Your endless love,
Then surely they would never cease to praise:

881

Debbye Graafsma.

LET EVERY TRIBE AND EVERY TONGUE
Bring praise to the Lamb,
For He has triumphed over all,
He has triumphed.
With His blood He has redeemed us
Forever to reign with Him in glory, amen.

We sing glory, glory to the Lamb;
Son of God, the Great I AM.
Awesome in splendour, triumphant King,
We give You praise and dominion over all.

Worthy, worthy is the Lamb;
Holy, resurrected Lamb.
Jesus, King Jesus, pre-eminent God,
We give You praise,
We give You praise over all.

882

Dave Bilbrough.

LET THE CHIMES OF FREEDOM RING
All across this earth;
Lift your voice in praise to Him
And sing of all His worth,
And sing of all His worth.

Open wide your prison doors
To greet the Lord of life;
Songs of triumph fill the air,
Christ Jesus is alive,
Christ Jesus is alive.

Let all the people hear the news
Of the One who comes to save:
He's the Lord of all the universe,
And forever He shall reign.

And forever more, yes forever more,
And forever more He will reign.
(Repeat)

In every corner of this earth,
To every tribe and tongue,
Make known that God so loved this world
That He gave His only Son,
He gave His only Son.

Spread the news and make it plain,
He breaks the power of sin;
Jesus died and He rose again,
His love will never end,
His love will never end.

He will return in majesty
To take His rightful place
As the King of all eternity,
The Name above all names,
The Name above all names.

883

Phil Wilthew.

LET THE CHURCH ARISE,
And let the darkness fall.
Say to those chains,
'You are now set free!'
Sickness has died its death
Through the blood of Christ.
To all the oppressed
He now promises life.

Jesus, Lord of all,
Come to us in a time of drought;
Send Your showers,
Let us know the riches of Your mercy.
Jesus, Lord of all,
Come to us in a time of need;
Send revival,
Let our nation see Your awesome glory.

Awake, O church,
Sing with all Your might;
The Lord of all the earth
Is in Your midst.
He is mending lives,
He is winning hearts;
In these coming days
Let revival start.

Come, let us go to the house of God,
With His praises in our hearts;
For the Lord has done great things for us,
And His glory's coming again.
(Repeat)

884

Bryn Haworth.

LET THE RIGHTEOUS SING,
Come let the righteous dance,
Rejoice before your God,
Be happy and joyful,
Give Him your praise.
We give You our praise.
Shout for joy to God
Who rides upon the clouds,
How awesome are His deeds,
So great is His power.
Give Him your praise.
We give You our praise.

He gives the desolate a home,
He leads the prisoners out with singing.
Father to the fatherless,
Defender of the widow
Is God in His holy place.

885

David Fellingham.

LET US DRAW NEAR to God
In full assurance of faith,
Knowing that as we draw near to Him,
He will draw near to us.
In the holy place
We stand in confidence,
Knowing our lives are cleansed in the blood of the Lamb,
We will worship and adore.

886 Mark Altrogge.

LET US DRAW NEAR WITH CONFIDENCE,
We have a Great High Priest.
There's mercy enough for all our sins,
We have a Great High Priest.
He was made weak and He was tried,
We have a Great High Priest.
He's able to feel and sympathise,
We have a Great High Priest.

He's the Lamb of God,
Slain before the ages,
The only Son,
The Servant crowned as King.
The One who came
To crush the works of darkness,
And He will fill all things, all things.

Let us each come with conscience cleansed,
We have a Great High Priest.
It's by His shed blood we enter in,
We have a Great High Priest.
We trust in no merits of our own,
We have a Great High Priest.
But look to the power of the cross alone,
We have a Great High Priest.

887 Paul Oakley.

LET US GO up to the house of God
With a shout of praise,
With a song of celebration.
We'll ascend the hill of the Lord,
We can stand in the holy place.

We can have clean hands and a pure heart;
His blood can cleanse us from all our unrighteousness.
He has made a way though the cross;
Jesus' blood was shed for us.
We can draw near to our God.

Now His body has been broken,
And the curtain torn in two.
We can enter by a new and living way
Before His throne.
Yes, we can fellowship with Him,
The King of glory, King of kings.

888

Noel & Tricia Richards.

Oh . . .
Oh . . .
Oh . . .
LET YOUR LOVE COME DOWN.
(Repeat)

There is violence in the air.
Fear touches all our lives.
How much pain can people bear?
Are we reaping what we've sown,
Voices silent for too long?
We are calling,
Let Your love come down.

There is power in Your love,
Bringing laughter out of tears.
It can heal the wounded soul.
In the streets where anger reigns
Love will wash away the pain.
We are calling,
Heaven's love come down.

889 David & Nathan Fellingham.

LET YOUR WORD run freely through this nation,
Strong Deliverer, break the grip of satan's power.
Let the cross of Jesus stand above the idols of this land,
Let anointed lives rise up and take their stand.

And we will glorify the Lamb,
Slain from eternity.
Jesus is Lord, we declare His name,
And stand in His victory,
And stand in His victory.

With prophetic words of power, expose the darkness;
With apostolic wisdom build the church.
With zeal for the lost let the story be told,
Let the shepherds feed the lambs within their folds.

Let the Holy Spirit's fire burn within us,
Cleansed from sin and pure within we stand upright.
Not yielding to wrong, we will live in holiness,
Bringing glory to the Saviour, we will shine.

890 Dave Bilbrough.

LIFT HIM UP, *lift Him high,*
Let His praises fill the sky.
Oh, heaven's gates are open wide
To those who hear the call.
(Repeat)

Through every generation
This truth will always shine,
That Christ came down among us,
Now He is glorified.

The message of the kingdom
Stands unshakeable through time:
That man can be forgiven,
If you seek then you will find.

891 Graham Kendrick.

LIKE A CANDLE FLAME,
Flickering small in our darkness.
Uncreated light
Shines through infant eyes.

God is with us, alleluia. (Men)
God is with us, alleluia. (Women)
Come to save us, alleluia. (Men)
Come to save us, (Women)
Alleluia! (All).

Stars and angels sing,
Yet the earth sleeps in shadows;
Can this tiny spark
Set a world on fire?

Yet His light shall shine
From our lives, Spirit blazing,
As we touch the flame
Of His holy fire.

892 Timothy Dudley-Smith.

LORD, FOR THE YEARS Your love has kept and guided,
Urged and inspired us, cheered us on our way,
Sought us and saved us, pardoned and provided:
Lord of the years, we bring our thanks today.

Lord, for that word, the word of life which fires us,
Speaks to our hearts and sets our souls ablaze,
Teaches and trains, rebukes us and inspires us:
Lord of the word, receive Your people's praise.

Lord, for our land in this our generation,
Spirits oppressed by pleasure, wealth and care:
For young and old, for commonwealth and nation,
Lord of our land, be pleased to hear our prayer.

Lord, for our world where men disown and doubt You,
Loveless in strength, and comfortless in pain,
Hungry and helpless, lost indeed without You:
Lord of the world, we pray that Christ may reign.

Lord for ourselves; in living power remake us –
Self on the cross and Christ upon the throne,
Past put behind us, for the future take us:
Lord of our lives, to live for Christ alone.

893

Dave Bilbrough.

LORD, HAVE MERCY,
Lord, have mercy:
Move in power on this land.
(Repeat)

Hear our prayer,
Hear our prayer,
O Lord, O Lord.
(Repeat)

894

Robert & Dawn Critchley.

LORD, I COME BEFORE YOUR THRONE OF GRACE;
I find rest in Your presence
And fulness of joy.
In worship and wonder
I behold Your face,
Singing what a faithful God have I.

What a faithful God have I,
What a faithful God.
What a faithful God have I,
Faithful in every way.

Lord of mercy, You have heard my cry;
Through the storm You're the beacon,
My song in the night.
In the shelter of Your wings,
Hear my heart's reply,
Singing what a faithful God have I.

Lord all sovereign, granting peace from heaven,
Let me comfort those who suffer
With the comfort You have given.
I will tell of Your great love for as long as I live,
Singing what a faithful God have I.

895

Geoff Bullock.

LORD, I COME TO YOU,
Let my heart be changed, renewed,
Flowing from the grace
That I found in You.
And Lord, I've come to know
The weaknesses I see in me
Will be stripped away
By the power of Your love.

Hold me close,
Let Your love surround me.
Bring me near, draw me to Your side.
And as I wait
I'll rise up like the eagle,
And I will soar with You,
Your Spirit leads me on
In the power of Your love.

Lord, unveil my eyes,
Let me see You face to face,
The knowledge of Your love
As You live in me.
Lord, renew my mind
As Your will unfolds in my life,
In living every day
By the power of Your love.

896

Brian Doerksen.

LORD, I HAVE HEARD OF YOUR FAME,
I stand in awe of Your deeds. O Lord,
I have heard of Your fame,
I stand in awe of Your deeds, O Lord.

Renew them, renew them,
In our day, and in our time
Make them known.
(Repeat)
In wrath remember mercy.

897

Rick Founds.

LORD, I LIFT YOUR NAME ON HIGH;
Lord, I love to sing Your praises.
I'm so glad You're in my life;
I'm so glad You came to save us.

You came from heaven to earth to show the way,
From the earth to the cross,
My debt to pay.
From the cross to the grave,
From the grave to the sky,
Lord, I lift Your name on high.

898

Stephen McPherson.

LORD, I LONG TO SEE YOU GLORIFIED
In everything I do;
All my heartfelt dreams I put aside,
To see Your Spirit move with power in my life.

Jesus, Lord of all eternity,
Your children rise in faith;
All the earth displays Your glory,
And each word You speak
Brings life to all who hear.

Lord of all,
All of creation sings Your praise
In heaven and earth.
Lord, we stand,
Hearts open wide,
Be exalted.

899

Rick Founds.

LORD, LOOK UPON MY NEED,
I need You, I need You.
Lord, have mercy now on me,
Forgive me, O Lord, forgive me,
And I will be clean.

O Lord, You are familiar with my ways,
There is nothing hid from You.
O Lord, You know the number of my days,
I want to live my life for You.

900 Darlene Zschech.

LORD, MY HEART CRIES OUT,
'Glory to the King';
My greatest love in life,
I hand You everything:
'Glory, glory',
I hear the angels sing.

Open my ears,
Let me hear Your voice,
To know that sweet sound,
Oh, my soul rejoice:
'Glory, glory',
I hear the angels sing.

You're the Father to the fatherless,
The answer to my dreams.
I see You crowned in righteousness,
We cry, 'Glory to the King'.
Comforter to the lonely,
The lifter of my head.
I see You veiled in majesty;
We cry, 'Glory, glory',
We cry, 'Glory to the King'.

901 Joe King.

LORD OF ALL CREATION,
Let this generation
See a visitation of Your power;
Put to flight all the powers of darkness,
O come, Lord Jesus, come.

Lord of all creation,
Let this generation
See a visitation of Your power.
Lord of all creation,
There's an expectation
Rising in this nation every hour.

Father God, forgive us,
Send Your cleansing rivers,
Wash us now and give us holy power;
Fill this land with Your awesome presence,
O come, Lord Jesus, come.

902

Jan Struther.

LORD OF ALL HOPEFULNESS,
Lord of all joy,
Whose trust, ever child-like,
No cares could destroy;
Be there at our waking,
And give us, we pray,
Your bliss in our hearts, Lord,
At the break of the day.

Lord of all eagerness, Lord of all faith,
Whose strong hands were skilled
At the plane and the lathe;
Be there at our labours,
And give us, we pray,
Your strength in our hearts, Lord,
At the noon of the day.

Lord of all kindliness, Lord of all grace,
Your hands swift to welcome,
Your arms to embrace;
Be there at our homing,
And give us, we pray,
Your love in our hearts, Lord,
At the eve of the day.

Lord of all gentleness, Lord of all calm,
Whose voice is contentment,
Whose presence is balm;
Be there at our sleeping,
And give us, we pray,
Your peace in our hearts, Lord,
At the end of the day.

903

Kevin Prosch.

LORD OF THE DANCE,
You're the dancing Lord.
(Repeat x4)
Everybody dance, yeah!

Well everybody dance, now,
Get in the Holy Ghost.
Everybody praise the One, love the One,
You want the One, yeah,
The One you want the most, now.
Can't nobody stop me now,
I'm gonna give it everything I've got.
I come to You, run to You,
Run to You, yeah,
Just like a child.

It's just this love I have inside,
Yeah, I want it.
I feel You pleasure in my heart,
Yeah, I need it.
I want Your love
More and more each day.
And when I dance before You, Lord,
I'm gonna dance with all my might.

904

Ray Goudie, Dave Bankhead & Steve Bassett.

LORD, POUR OUT YOUR SPIRIT
On all the peoples of the earth;
Let Your sons and daughters
Speak Your words of prophecy.
Send us dreams and visions,
Reveal the secrets of Your heart;
Lord, our faith is rising,
Let all heaven sound the coming of Your day.

There's gonna be a great awakening,
There's gonna be a great revival in our land.
There's gonna be a great awakening,
And everyone who calls on Jesus,
They will be saved.

Lord, pour out Your Spirit
On all the nations of the world;
Let them see Your glory,
Let them fall in reverent awe.
Show Your mighty power,
Shake the heavens and the earth;
Lord, the world is waiting,
Let creation see the coming of Your day.

905

Dave Bilbrough.

LORD, WE COME IN ADORATION,
Lay our lives before You now.
We are here to reach the nations,
To tell the world of Jesus' power.
We would seek Your awesome glory,
All the gifts that You endow;
Called to reach this generation,
And now is the appointed hour.

We will go in Your name;
Go and proclaim Your kingdom.
Go in Your name,
For we have been chosen to tell all creation
That Jesus is King of all kings.

We believe that You have spoken
Through Your Son to all the earth;
Given us this great commission
To spread the news of all Your worth.
Set apart to serve You only,
Let our lives display Your love;
Hearts infused that tell the story
Of God come down from heaven above.

Grant to us a fresh anointing,
Holy Spirit, be our guide;
Satisfy our deepest longing—
Jesus Christ be glorified.
Every tribe and every people,
Hear the message that we bring;
Christ has triumphed over evil,
Bow the knee and worship Him.

906

David Fellingham.

LORD, WE CRY TO YOU: God, break through!
Let Your presence come in revival.
Like the gentle dew, our lives renew;
Let Your presence come in revival.

(Men) *O God, break through!*
(Women) *Send Your Spirit, Lord.*
(Men) *O God, break through!*
(Women) *Send Your Spirit.*
(All) *Let the name of Jesus be proclaimed.*
(Repeat)
(All) *O God, break through.*

Lord, we cry to You: God break through!
Move upon Your church in revival.
Like a mighty wind and tongues of fire,
Let Your Spirit come in revival.

Lord, we cry to You: God, break through!
Sweep across this land in revival.
Like the mighty rain, flood this land again;
Let Your power come in revival.

907

Richard Lewis.

LORD, WE LONG TO SEE YOUR GLORY,
Gaze upon Your lovely face.
Holy Spirit, come among us,
Lead us to that secret place.

Holy God,
We long to see Your glory,
To touch Your holy majesty, O Lord.
Holy God,
Let us stay in Your presence,
And worship at Your feet forever more.
Holy God.
Holy God.

908

Nathan Fellingham.

LORD, WE LONG TO SEE YOUR GLORY,
Lord, we long to feel Your power.
In these times of refreshing,
We long to know You more.
To behold You in Your majesty,
Our hearts are filled with joy;
As we look towards the coming King,
We cry 'Lord, let Your glory fall.'

There'll be a day when we will reign with Him,
The Bride of Christ born for perfect unity with Him.
We shall see Him face to face,
But until that day we shall pray,
'Show us Your glory.'

Help us to sing like the angels sing.
Help us to praise in the courts of our King.
Help us to dance like David danced,
Stirred by the love of Your Son,
Stirred by the love of Your Son.

909

Ian Smale.

LORD, WE'VE COME TO WORSHIP YOU,
Lord, we've come to praise:
Lord, we've come to worship You
In oh, so many ways.
Some of us shout,
And some of us sing,
And some of us whisper the praise we bring;
But Lord, we all are gathering
To give to You our praise.

910

Judy Pruett.

LORD, YOU ARE THE AUTHOR OF MY LIFE,
You have begun a work in me,
You have predestined me
To do Your perfect will.
And Lord, You are the Lord of all my days,
You are the Lord of all my nights,
You have chosen me
To carry forth Your word.

So Lord, finish in me what You've begun,
Guide me by Your mighty hand, Lord:
Let me trust in You.
And Lord, let me seek Your holy face,
May I always walk with You, Lord,
And let Your will be done.

911

David Baroni.

LORD, YOU ARE WORTHY,
Lord, You are worthy,
Lord, You are worthy,
We give You praise.

Lord, You are worthy...

Lord, You are holy...

Lord, we adore You...

Lord, You are worthy...

912

Martin Smith.

LORD, YOU HAVE MY HEART,
And I will search for Yours;
Jesus, take my life and lead me on.
Lord, You have my heart,
And I will search for Yours;
Let me be to You a sacrifice.

And I will praise you, Lord. *(Men)*
I will praise You, Lord. *(Women)*
And I will sing of love come down. *(Men)*

I will sing of love come down. *(Women)*
And as You show Your face, *(Men)*
Show Your face, *(Women)*
We'll see Your glory here. *(All)*

913

Wayne Drain.

LOST IN THE SHUFFLE,
I was lost as a goose,
The devil had a rope out,
And it looked just like a noose.
But just before I went off of that deep end,
My Father threw me out a line,
Forgave me of my sin.

Now we're dancin', me and the Father,
He's throwing me up in the air.
We're dancin', me and the Father,
He's swinging me,
I like it up there with my Father,
I like it up there with my Father.

He took me to the water,
And He cleaned me real good,
Then He raised me up to be with Him,
I feel just like I should.
He filled me with His Spirit,
I drank the whole cup,
Now when He calls I hear it,
Hey, turn that volume up!

'Cause we're dancin'...

God's got a big family, more than anyone can count;
There's always room for one more,
No need to be left out.
So come on, come on, come on,

And you could be dancin', you and the Father,
He'll throw you up in the air.
You'll be dancin', you and the Father,
He'll swing you up,
You'll like it up there with the Father,
You'll like it up there with the Father.

914

Noel & Tricia Richards.

LOVE SONGS FROM HEAVEN are filling the earth,
Bringing great hope to all nations.
Evil has prospered, but truth is alive;
In this dark world the light still shines.

Nothing has silenced this gospel of Christ;
It echoes down through the ages.
Blood of the martyrs has made Your church strong;
In this dark world the light still shines.

For You we live,
And for You we may die;
Through us may Jesus be seen.
For You alone we will offer our lives;
In this dark world our light will shine.

Let every nation be filled with Your song:
This is the cry of Your people.
We will not settle for anything less,
In this dark world our light must shine.

915

Graham Kendrick.

MAGNIFICENT WARRIOR, arrayed for battle,
We see You ready to slay Your enemies.
O Mighty Captain of heaven's armies,
We bow before You, we worship You.

So take Your sword upon Your side
O Mighty One, clothe Yourself
With splendour and with majesty,
And in Your majesty ride forth.
Ride forth victoriously for truth.
Humility and righteousness.
Let Your strong right hand
Display Your awesome deeds.

Magnificent Warrior, we hear Your strong command
To join the ranks of light and march into the fight;
By faith to overthrow ten thousand Jerichos,
To make Your judgements known in all the earth.

916 Russell Fragar.

MAKES YOU WANNA DANCE, *(echo)*
Makes you wanna sing, *(echo)*
Makes you wanna shout all about it,
Shout all about it,
Shout it that Jesus is King.
(Repeat)

Every nation, power and tongue
Will bow down to Your name;
Every eye will see,
Every ear will hear Your name proclaimed,
This is gonna be our cry
Until You come again:
'Jesus is the only name
By which man can be saved.'

All over the world people just like us
Are calling Your name, living in Your love.
All over the world people just like us
Are following Jesus.
(Repeat)

(Last time)
We're worshipping Jesus,
We're following Jesus,
We're worshipping Jesus,
We're calling on Jesus.

917

Daniel Brymer.

MAKE US A HOUSE OF PRAYER,
That we might meet You there,
On behalf of the nation,
To a dying generation,
Make us a house of prayer.

And Lord, teach us to pray
Unceasingly night and day.
Make our intercession
For You a mighty weapon.
O Lord, teach us to pray.

918

Ian White.

MAY GOD BE GRACIOUS TO US and bless us,
Make His face to shine upon us.
May Your ways be known over the earth
And Your salvation among all nations.

May the peoples praise You;
O God, may all the peoples praise You.
May the peoples praise You;
O God, may all the peoples praise You.

May the nations be glad and sing for joy,
For with justice You rule the people You guide.
May Your ways be known over all the earth,
And Your salvation among all nations.

Then the harvest will come to the land,
And God, our God, will bless us.
God will bless us, and all the ends
Of earth will fear Him.

919

David Gate.

MAY I SING A SONG OF LOVE
To the One who saved my soul?
May I bow my head today
In the presence of the King?

You have called and I will come,
Lift my hands up to Your throne;
Worship You on holy ground –
That's what I long to do.

Draw me near into Your heart.
All I have is broken love,
And a thirst that cries for more.
Draw me near to You.

920

Chris Bowater.

MAY OUR WORSHIP BE AS FRAGRANCE,
May our worship be as incense poured forth,
May our worship be acceptable
As a living sacrifice,
As a living sacrifice.

We are willing to pay the price,
We are willing to lay down our lives
As an offering of obedience,
As a living sacrifice,
As a living sacrifice.

921

MEN OF FAITH, rise up and sing
Of the great and glorious King;
You are strong when you feel weak,
In your brokenness complete.

Shout to the north and the south,
Sing to the east and the west:
Jesus is Saviour to all,
Lord of heaven and earth.

(Last time)
Lord of heaven and earth,
Lord of heaven and earth,
Lord of heaven and earth.

Rise up women of the truth,
Stand and sing to broken hearts,
Who can know the healing power
Of our glorious King of love.

We've been through fire,
We've been through rain;
We've been refined
By the power of His name.
We've fallen deeper in love with You,
You've burned the truth on our lips.

Rise up church with broken wings;
Fill this place with songs again,
Of our God who reigns on high:
By His grace again we'll fly.

922

John Chisum & Gary Sadler.

MERCIFUL GOD AND FATHER,
Loving us like no other,
Hear our prayer, the cry of our hearts,
As we come to You.
We acknowledge our transgressions,
We confess to You our sins;
Show us mercy and compassion,
Touch our lives
With Your healing grace again.

Release us from the past,
As we seek Your face.
Wash us free at last,
We receive Your love,
We receive Your healing grace.
We receive Your love,
We receive Your healing grace.

923

Chris Bowater and Mark & Helen Johnson.

MIGHTY GOD,
Everlasting Father,
Wonderful Counsellor,
You're the Prince of Peace.
(Repeat)

You are Lord of heaven,
You are called Emmanuel;
God is now with us,
Ever present to deliver.
You are God eternal,
You are Lord of all the earth;
Love has come to us,
Bringing us new birth.

A light to those in darkness,
And a guide to paths of peace;
Love and mercy dawns,
Grace, forgiveness and salvation.
Light for revelation,
Glory to Your people;
Son of the Most High,
God's love gift to all.

924 Eugene Greco, Gerrit Gustafson, Don Moen

MIGHTY IS OUR GOD,
Mighty is our King;
Mighty is our Lord,
Ruler of everything.
Glory to our God,
Glory to our King;
Glory to our Lord,
Ruler of everything.

His name is higher,
Higher than any other name;
His power is greater,
For He has created everything.

925 A. P. Douglas.

MIGHTY IS THE LORD and most worthy of praise,
Praise Him all you people.
Look upon Him, God alone who saves:
Praise the Lord of all.
Nations will rise and nations will fall,
Praise Him all you people.
But there is One who is Lord of all:
Praise the Lord of all.

He is Wonderful, Counsellor,
Glorious Prince of Peace.
He is Lord and King of everything,
His praises never cease.
(Repeat)

Awesome and great, like the strongest tower,
Praise Him all you people.
He is the one with limitless power,
Praise the Lord of all.
Leaders may come and presidents fall,
Praise Him all you people.
But there is One who is Lord of all:
Praise the Lord of all.

926

Carol Owen.

MIGHTY, MIGHTY LORD.
Precious is Your name.
Wonderful Your ways,
Worthy of all praise, Jehovah.

Mighty, mighty Lord.
Holy is Your name.
Glorious and true,
Great in all You do, Jehovah,
Jehovah.

Hallowed be Your name,
Lord God Almighty,
For Yours is the kingdom,
The power and the glory,
Forever more.

927

Brian Doerksen.

MORE THAN OXYGEN, I need Your love;
More than life-giving food
The hungry dream of.
More than an eloquent word
Depends on the tongue;
More than a passionate song
Needs to be sung.

More than a word could ever say,
More than a song could ever convey;
I need You more than all of these things.
Father, I need You more.

More than magnet and steel
Are drawn to unite;
More that poets love words
To rhyme as they write.
More than comforting warmth
Of sun in spring;
More than the eagle loves wind
Under its wings.

More than a blazing fire
On a winter's night;
More than tall evergreens
Reach for the light.
More than the pounding waves
Long for the shore;
More than these gifts You give,
I love You more.

928

Steve & Vikki Cook.

MOST HOLY JUDGE,
I stood before You guilty,
When you sent Jesus to the cross for my sin.
There Your love was revealed,
Your justice vindicated,
One sacrifice has paid the cost
For all who trust in Jesus.

Now I'm justified,
You declare me righteous,
Justified by the blood of the Lamb.
Justified freely by Your mercy,
By faith I stand and I'm justified.

I come to You,
And I can call you 'Father',
There is no fear
There is no shame before You.
For by Your gift of grace
Now I am one of Your children,
An heir with those who bear Your name,
And share the hope of glory.

929

Author unknown.

MUKTI DILAYE *Yesu naam,*
Shanti dilaye Yesu naam.
(Repeat)
(Peace comes to you in Jesus' name,
Salvation in no other name.)

Yesu daya ka behta sagar
Yesu daya ka behta sagar
Yesu hai data mahan
Yesu hai data mahan
(Jesus is the Ocean of Grace:
You are majestic, Lord.)

Charni main tooney janamliya Yesu
Charni main tooney janamliya Yesu
Sooley pay kiya vishram
Sooley pay kiya vishram
(Jesus, You were born in a manger (Made of wood:)
You were crucified on the cross (Made of wood.))

Peace comes to you in Jesus' name,
Salvation in no other name.

Ham sab key papon ko mitane
Ham sab key papon ko mitane
Yesu hua hai balidan
Yesu hua hai balidan
(For the remission of our sins,
Jesus has been sacrificed on the cross.)

Krus par apna khoon bahaa kar
Krus par apna khoon bahaa kar
Sara chukaya daam
Sara chukaya daam
(By shedding Your blood on the cross,
You paid the full price for our sins.)

930

Stuart Townend.

MY FIRST LOVE is a blazing fire,
I feel His powerful love in me.
For He has kindled a flame of passion,
And I will let it grow in me.
And in the night I will sing Your praise, my love.
And in the morning I'll seek Your face, my love.

And like a child I will dance in Your presence,
Oh, let the joy of heaven pour down on me.
I still remember the first day I met You,
And I don't ever want to lose that fire,
My first love.

My first love is a rushing river,
A waterfall that will never cease;
And in the torrent of tears and laughter,
I feel a healing power released.
And I will draw from Your well of life, my love,
And in Your grace I'll be satisfied, my love.

Restore the years of the church's slumber,
Revive the fire that has grown so dim;
Renew the love of those first encounters,
That we may come alive again.
And we will rise like the dawn throughout the
earth,
Until the trumpet announces Your return.

931

Ian Smale.

MY GOD SHALL SUPPLY ALL MY NEEDS,
My God shall supply all my needs,
My God shall supply all my needs
'Cause it says so in the Bible.
'Cause it says so (where?)
In the book that came from heaven,
'Cause it says so (where?)
Isaiah fifty-eight eleven.
My God shall supply all my needs
'Cause it says so in the Bible.

932

Chris Williams.

MY HEART,
I want to give You my heart,
In service to the Lord, the One who cares
To ask for my life.
Take me,

Mould my life and make me
Into a child who longs to stay by Your side
And learn of Your ways.

For when I sought You, Lord, You heard me,
You delivered me from fear;
And by Your grace and mercy
You have brought us both so near.
I want to kneel before Your feet, Lord,
And to gaze upon Your face;
For the God who asks for my life
Loves me completely and always.

933

Maggi Dawn.

MY HEART IS NOT RAISED UP TOO HIGH,
My eyes don't search beyond the sky.
I do not seek what can't be known,
Nor fret myself over mysteries.

But I have calmed and soothed my soul,
Like a child at rest in its mother's arms;
Like this child sleeping by my side,
My soul, in God, knows peace and calm.

All you who love and trust your God,
In this God shall you put your hope,
For there you'll find unfailing love,
From this time forth, and forever more.

934

Tim Hughes.

MY JESUS, MY LIFELINE,
I need You more than I've ever known.
There's no one quite like You,
I'm crying out for Your loving.

Oh Jesus, oh Jesus,
I've never known a love like this before.
Oh Jesus, oh Jesus,
Accept this love I give to You,
It's all I can do.

I'm searching, I'm longing,
Please meet me just as You want to.
I'll stand here to offer,
Offer up this song of love to You.

935

Darlene Zschech.

MY JESUS, MY SAVIOUR,
Lord, there is none like You.
All of my days I want to praise
The wonders of Your mighty love.
My comfort, my shelter,
Tower of refuge and strength,
Let every breath, all that I am,
Never cease to worship You.

Shout to the Lord all the earth, let us sing
Power and majesty, praise to the King.
Mountains bow down
And the seas will roar
At the sound of Your name.
I sing for joy at the work of Your hands.
Forever I'll love You, forever I'll stand.
Nothing compares to the
Promise I have in You.

936

Daniel Gardner.

MY LIFE IS IN YOU, LORD,
My strength is in You, Lord,
My hope is in You, Lord,
In You, it's in You.
(Repeat)

(Last time)
In You.

I will praise You with all of my life;
I will praise You with all of my strength.
With all of my life,
With all of my strength;
All of my hope is in You.

937

Noel & Tricia Richards.

MY LIPS SHALL PRAISE YOU,
My great Redeemer;
My heart will worship
Almighty Saviour.

You take all my guilt away,
Turn the darkest night to brightest day,
You are the restorer of my soul.

Love that conquers every fear,
In the midst of trouble You draw near,
You are the restorer of my soul.

You're the source of happiness,
Bringing peace when I am in distress,
You are the restorer of my soul.

938

Laurie Jasurda.

MY TRUST IS IN THE NAME OF THE LORD
Who made heaven and earth;
My trust is in the name of the Lord
Who made heaven and earth.

Sing hallelujah, hallelujah.
Hallelujah, hallelu, hallelujah.

My hope is in the name of the Lord ...

My joy is in the name of the Lord ...

939

Timothy Dudley-Smith.

NAME OF ALL MAJESTY,
Fathomless mystery,
King of the ages
By angels adored;
Power and authority,
Splendour and dignity,
Bow to His mastery –
Jesus is Lord!

Child of our destiny,
God from eternity,
Love of the Father
On sinners outpoured;
See now what God has done,
Sending His only Son,
Christ the belovèd One –
Jesus is Lord!

Saviour of Calvary,
Costliest victory,
Darkness defeated
And Eden restored;

Born as a man to die,
Nailed to a cross on high,
Cold in the grave to lie –
Jesus is Lord!

Source of all sovereignty,
Light, immortality,
Life everlasting
And heaven assured;
So with the ransomed, we
Praise Him eternally,
Christ in His majesty –
Jesus is Lord!

940

Sarah Flower Adams.

NEARER, MY GOD, TO THEE,
Nearer to Thee:
E'en though it be a cross
That raiseth me,
Still all my song would be,
Nearer, my God, to Thee,
Nearer to Thee, nearer to Thee.

Though, like the wanderer,
The sun gone down,
Darkness be over me,
My rest a stone,
Yet in my dreams I'd be
Nearer, my God, to Thee,
Nearer to Thee, nearer to Thee.

There let the way appear,
Steps up to heaven;
All that Thou sendest me,
In mercy given;
Angels to beckon me
Nearer, my God, to Thee,
Nearer to Thee, nearer to Thee.

Then, with my waking thoughts
Bright with Thy praise,
Out of my stony griefs
Bethel I'll raise;
So by my woes to be
Nearer, my God, to Thee,
Nearer to Thee, nearer to Thee.

Or, if on joyful wing
Cleaving the sky,
Sun, moon, and stars forgot,
Upwards I fly,
Still all my song shall be,
Nearer, my God, to Thee,
Nearer to Thee, nearer to Thee.

941

Chris Roe.

NEVER LET MY HEART GROW COLD.
Lord, help my to love You
With a love that never dies.
Set my heart ablaze with burning desire
To see Jesus glorified,
To see Jesus glorified.

942

David Fellingham.

NEW COVENANT PEOPLE rejoice,
Lift up your eyes and see your King.
Reigning in power on His heavenly throne,
Angels are joyfully singing:

To the Father, our Creator,
To our Judge and Lord.
And to Jesus, Mediator,
Who has cleansed us in His blood.

Let us through Jesus draw near to God,
Offering up our sacrifice,
Confessing that Jesus is Lord over all,
Joining with heavenly praises:

We give thanks to You with fear,
Holy God, consuming fire,
Confessing that Jesus is Lord over all,
We bring our love and devotion:

943

Mark Altrogge.

NO EYE HAS SEEN,
And no ear has heard,
And no mind has ever conceived
The glorious things
That You have prepared
For everyone who has believed;
You brought us near and You called us Your own,
And made us joint heirs with Your Son.

How high and how wide,
How deep and how long,
How sweet and how strong is Your love;
How lavish Your grace,
How faithful Your ways,
How great is Your love, O Lord.

Objects of mercy,
Who should have known wrath,
We're filled with unspeakable joy;
Riches of wisdom
Unsearchable wealth,
And the wonder of knowing Your voice.
You are our treasure and our great reward,
Our hope and our glorious King.

944

Paul & Rita Baloche & Ed Kerr.

NO EYE HAS SEEN, NO EAR HAS HEARD,
No mind has conceived what the Lord has prepared;
But by His Spirit, He has revealed
His plan to those who love Him.
(Repeat)

We've been held by His everlasting love,
Led with loving kindness by His hand;
We have hope for the future yet to come,
In time we'll understand the mystery of His plan.

945

Carol Owen.

NO ONE IS LIKE YOU, O LORD;
You are great and Your name is mighty.
No one is like You, O Lord;
You are great and Your name is mighty.
Who should not revere You,
O King of the nations?
Who should not revere You,
For this is Your due?
Among all wise men
In all of their kingdoms,
There is none like You.

No one is like You, O Lord;
You're enthroned over all the nations.
No one is like You, O Lord;
You're enthroned over all the nations.
Who should not revere You,
O King of the nations?
Who should not revere You,
For this is Your due?

Among all the wise men
In all of their kingdoms,
There is none like You.

None like You, O Lord,
The King and the Creator.
None like You, O Lord,
Our Father and our Maker.
None like You, O Lord,
Your faithfulness surrounds You.
How majestic is Your name,
As Your people we proclaim:

946

Robert Gay.

NO OTHER NAME but the name of Jesus,
No other name but the name of the Lord;
No other name but the name of Jesus
Is worthy of glory, and worthy of honour,
And worthy of power and all praise.

His name is exalted far above the earth,
His name is high above the heavens;
His name is exalted far above the earth,
Give glory and honour and praise unto His name.

947

Noel & Tricia Richards.

NOTHING SHALL SEPARATE US
From the love of God.
Nothing shall separate us
From the love of God.

God did not spare His only Son,
Gave Him to save us all.
Sin's price was met by Jesus' death
And heaven's mercy falls.

Up from the grave Jesus was raised
To sit at God's right hand;
Pleading our cause in heaven's courts,
Forgiven we can stand.

Now by God's grace we have embraced
A life set free from sin;
We shall deny all that destroys
Our union with Him.

948

Tom Dowell.

NO WEAPON FORMED, or army or king,
Shall be able to stand
Against the Lord and His anointed.
(Repeat)

All principalities and powers
Shall crumble before the Lord;
And men's hearts shall be released,
And they shall come unto the Lord.

No weapon formed, or army or king,
Shall be able to stand
Against the Lord and His anointed.

949

Alfred Vine.

O BREATH OF GOD, BREATHE ON US NOW,
And move within us while we pray;
The Spring of our new life art Thou,
The very light of our new day.

O strangely art Thou with us, Lord,
Neither in height nor depth to seek:
In nearness shall Thy voice be heard;
Spirit to spirit Thou dost speak.

Christ is our Advocate on high;
Thou art our Advocate within.
O plead the truth, and make reply
To every argument of sin.

But ah, this faithless heart of mine,
The way I know, I know my Guide;
Forgive me, O my Friend divine,
That I so often turn aside.

Be with me when no other friend
The mystery of my heart can share;
And be Thou known, when fears transcend,
By Thy best name of Comforter.

950

Graham Kendrick.

O FATHER OF THE FATHERLESS,
In whom all families are blessed,
I love the way You father me.
You gave me life, forgave the past,
Now in Your arms I'm safe at last,
I love the way You father me.

Father me, forever You'll father me,
And in Your embrace I'll be forever secure.
I love the way You father me.
I love the way You father me.

When bruised and broken I draw near
You hold me close and dry my tears,
I love the way You father me.
At last my fearful heart is still,
Surrendered to Your perfect will,
I love the way You father me.

If in my foolishness I stray,
Returning empty and ashamed,
I love the way You father me.
Exchanging for my wretchedness
Your radiant robes of righteousness,
I love the way You father me.

And when I look into Your eyes
From deep within my spirit cries,
I love the way You father me.
Before such love I stand amazed
And ever will through endless days,
I love the way You father me.

951 William Cowper.

O FOR A CLOSER WALK WITH GOD,
A calm and heavenly frame,
A light to shine upon the road
That leads me to the Lamb.

Where is the blessèdness I knew
When I first saw the Lord?
Where is that soul-refreshing view
Of Jesus and His word?

What peaceful hours I once enjoyed!
How sweet their memory still!
But they have left an aching void
The world can never fill.

Return, O holy Dove! return,
Sweet messenger of rest!
I hate the sins that made Thee mourn,
And drove Thee from my breast.

The dearest idol I have known,
Whate'er that idol be,
Help me tear if from Thy throne,
And worship only Thee.

So shall my walk be close with God,
Calm and serene my frame;
So purer light shall mark the road
That leads me to the Lamb.

952

John Paculabo.

O GOD, BE MY STRENGTH
Through my doubt and my fear.
O God, be my comfort
When darkness is near.
O Lord of all hope,
You're my Saviour and Guide.
O Lord, have mercy on me.

O God of all mercy
And God of all grace,
Whose infinite gift
Was to die in my place,
Eternal Creator,
Redeemer and Friend,
O Lord, have mercy on me.

O God of all power,
Invisible King,
Restorer of man,
My life I bring,
O Lord of my heart,
Grant Your peace now I pray:
O Lord, have mercy on me.

953

Michael Perry.

O GOD BEYOND ALL PRAISING,
We worship You today,
And sing the love amazing
That songs cannot repay;
For we can only wonder
At every gift you send,
At blessings without number
And mercies without end:
We lift our hearts before You
And wait upon Your word,
We honour and adore You,
Our great and mighty Lord.

Then hear, O gracious Saviour,
Accept the love we bring,
That we who know Your favour
May serve You as our King;
And whether our tomorrows
Be filled with good or ill,
We'll triumph through our sorrows
And rise to bless You still:
To marvel at Your beauty
And glory in Your ways,
And make a joyful duty
Our sacrifice of praise!

954

Jamie Owens-Collins.

O GOD, MOST HIGH, Almighty King,
The Champion of heaven, Lord of everything;
You've fought, You've won, death's lost its sting,
And standing in Your victory we sing.

You have broken the chains
That held our captive souls.
You have broken the chains

And used them on Your foes.
All Your enemies are bound,
They tremble at the sound of Your name;
Jesus, You have broken the chains.

The power of hell has been undone,
Captivity held captive by the risen One,
And in the name of God's great Son,
We claim the mighty victory You've won.

955

William Booth.
Adpt. Lex Loizides.

O GOD OF BURNING, CLEANSING FLAME:
Send the fire!
Your blood-bought gift today we claim:
Send the fire today!
Look down and see this waiting host,
And send the promised Holy Ghost;
We need another Pentecost!
Send the fire today!
Send the fire today!

God of Elijah, hear our cry:
Send the fire!
And make us fit to live or die:
Send the fire today!
To burn up every trace of sin,
To bring the light and glory in,
The revolution now begin!
Send the fire today!
Send the fire today!

It's fire we want, for fire we plead:
Send the fire!
The fire will meet our every need:
Send the fire today!
For strength to always do what's right,

For grace to conquer in the fight,
For power to walk the world in white:
Send the fire today!
Send the fire today!

To make our weak hearts strong and brave:
Send the fire!
To live, a dying world to save:
Send the fire today!
Oh, see us on Your altar lay,
We give our lives to you today,
So crown the offering now we pray:
Send the fire today!
Send the fire today!
Send the fire today!

956

Martin Smith.

OH, LEAD ME
To the place where I can find You.
Oh, lead me
To the place where You'll be.

Lead me to the cross
Where we first met;
Draw me to my knees,
So we can talk.
Let me feel Your breath,
Let me know You're here with me.

957

Alan Rose.

OH, OUR LORD AND KING,
Our praise to You we bring,
There is no other Rock but You.

Seated high above,
You are the One we love,
This is our song of praise to You.

King forever!
You are the First and You're the Last.
You are sovereign;
All Your commands will always
Come to pass, to give You glory!

Who is like You?
Who else is worthy of pur praise?
We exalt You;
You reign in majesty and
Awesome splendour,
King forever!

Abba Father,
Your steadfast love will never fail.
You are faithful,
You are God and I will
Worship in Your
Courts for ever.

958

Geoff Bullock.

OH, THE MERCY OF GOD, the glory of grace,
That You chose to redeem us, to forgive and restore,
And You call us Your children, chosen in Him
To be holy and blameless to the glory of God.

To the praise of His glorious grace,
To the praise of His glory and power;
To Him be all glory, honour and praise
Forever and ever and ever, amen.

Oh, the richness of grace, the depths of His love,
In Him is redemption, the forgiveness of sin.
You called us as righteous, predestined in Him
For the praise of His glory, included in Christ.

Oh, the glory of God expressed in His Son,
His image and likeness revealed to us all;
The plea of the ages completed in Christ,
That we be presented perfected in Him.

959

Craig Musseau.

O LORD, ARISE, release Your power,
Scatter Your foes this very hour.
May we hold on to Your holy commands.
You are the Lord of every man.

You hold our lives, You give us breath,
You freed us from the power of death.
You're our salvation, our only hope,
You are the Lord of every man.

Your voice, it is like thunder
Over the waters.
Your voice echoes throughout the earth,
We will bow to the sound,
We will bow to the sound
Of Your voice.

960

Chris DuPré.

O LORD, HOW I LOVE TO SING YOUR PRAISES.
O Lord, how I love to dance for You.
O Lord, You have captured my affection,
Forever I will sing of Your love,
Forever I will bring to You my life,
Forever I will worship You.

And when I think of what You've done,
It makes me shout for joy.
And when I think of what's to come,
Living forever in Your presence,
Face to face with my magnificent obsession,
Forever, forever I will be with You.

Oh, la, la, la ...
Oh, la, la, la ...
Oh, la, la, la ...
Forever, forever I will be with You.

961

Andy Park.

O LORD I WANT TO SING YOUR PRAISES,
I want to praise Your name every day.
O Lord I want to sing Your praises,
I want to praise Your name every day.

Alleluia, allelu.
Alleluia, allelu.
(Alleluia.)

God, You are my God, and I will seek You;
I am satisfied when I find Your love.
God, You are my God, and I will seek You;
I am satisfied when I find Your love.

And I will praise You as long as I live,
For Your love is better than life.
In Your name I will lift up my hands,
For Your love is better than life.

962

Michael W. Smith.

O LORD OUR LORD,
How majestic is Your name in all the earth.
O Lord our Lord,
How majestic is Your name in all the earth.
O Lord, we praise Your name;
O Lord, we magnify Your name.
Prince of Peace,
Mighty God,
O Lord God Almighty.

963

Jon Soper, Mark Robinson & John Peters.

O LORD, YOU ARE MY ROCK AND MY REDEEMER;
My song, You are the Strength of my life.
O Lord, You are the Shepherd of Your people;
You keep us always walking in Your light.

You brought me out of darkness,
You took away my shame;
You broke the chains that bound me,
I praise Your name!

You carry all my sorrows,
You carry all my pain;
You fill me with Your Spirit,
I praise Your name!

964

Ian Smale.

O LORD, YOU'RE GREAT, You are fabulous,
We love You more than any words can sing, sing, sing.
O Lord, You're great, You are so generous,
You lavish us with gifts when we don't deserve a thing.

Allelu, alleluia, praise You, Lord.
Alleluia, praise You, Lord.
Alleluia, praise You, Lord.
(Repeat)

O Lord, You're great, You are so powerful,
You hold the mighty universe in Your hand, hand, hand.
O Lord, You're great, You are so beautiful,
You've poured out Your love on this undeserving land.

965

Maggi Dawn.

ONLY ONE THING I ask of the Lord:
Only one thing do I desire:
That I may dwell, may dwell in God's house
All of the days of my life,
All of the days of my life.

Even when days of trouble may come,
I will be safe if God is my home,
For I will hide in the shelter of love
All of the days of my life,
All of the days of my life.

I'll gaze on His beauty,
And sing of His glory;
While I have life within me,
What more could I need?

(Descant)
I'll sing to His holy name,
Forever He is the same,
His faithfulness never change,
Let all of the earth proclaim,
All of the days of my life.

966

Ian White.

OPEN THE DOORS OF PRAISE.
Open the doors of praise.
Open the doors of praise
And let the Lord come in.
(Repeat)

In the spirit world
There's a battle going on,
And it rages endlessly.
But in the name of the Lord,
We can stand on His word,
For in Him we have the victory.

For He lives in the praises of His people, *(echo)*
Here among us to empower us!

And the demons will flee,
As He said it would be,
And the skies will ring with shouts of praise.
And the Lord Jesus Christ
Will be lifted high,
The Holy One who truly saves!

For He lives . . .

967

Maldwyn Pope.

O RIGHTEOUS GOD who searches minds and hearts,
Bring to an end the violence of my foes,
And make the righteous more secure,
O righteous God.

Sing praise to the name of the Lord most high.
Sing praise to the name of the Lord most high.
Give thanks to the Lord who rescues me,
O righteous God.

O Lord my God, I take refuge in You;
Save and deliver me from all my foes.
My shield is God the Lord most high,
O Lord my God.

968

Samuel Trevor Francis.

O THE DEEP, DEEP LOVE OF JESUS!
Vast, unmeasured, boundless, free;
Rolling as a mighty ocean
In its fulness over me.
Underneath me, all around me,
Is the current of Thy love;
Leading onward, leading homeward,
To my glorious rest above.

O the deep, deep love of Jesus!
Spread His praise from shore to shore,
How He loveth, ever loveth,
Changeth never, nevermore;
How He watches o'er His loved ones,
Died to call them all His own;
How for them He intercedeth,
Watches over them from the throne.

O the deep, deep love of Jesus!
Love of every love the best:
'Tis an ocean vast of blessing,
'Tis a haven sweet of rest.
O the deep, deep love of Jesus!
'Tis a heaven of heavens to me;
And it lifts me up to glory,
For it lifts me up to Thee.

969 Brian Doerksen & Michael Hansen.

OUR FATHER IN HEAVEN,
Holy is Your name.
Forgive us our sins, Lord,
As we forgive.
Our Father in heaven,
Give us our bread.
Lead us not into temptation,
But deliver us from the evil one.

Your kingdom come, Your will be done.
Your kingdom come, Your will be done

On the earth as it is in heaven.
Let it be done on the earth.
Amen. Amen.

970 Keith Routledge.

OUR FATHER IN HEAVEN,
Hallowed be Your name,
Your kingdom come,
Your will be done on earth as in heaven.
Give us today our daily bread,
And forgive us our sins
As we forgive those who sin against us,
And lead us not into temptation,
But deliver us from evil;

For the kingdom, the power,
And the glory are Yours,
Now and forever, Amen.

(Last time)
For the kingdom, the power
And the glory are Yours,
Now and forever,
Now and forever,
Now and forever, Amen.

971

Noel & Tricia Richards.

OUR GOD IS AWESOME IN POWER,
Scatters His enemies;
Our God is mighty in bringing
The powerful to their knees.
He has put on His armour,
He is prepared for war;
Mercy and justice triumph
When the Lion of Judah roars.

The Lord is a warrior,
We will march with Him.
The Lord is a warrior,
Leading us to win.
(Repeat)

Waken the warrior spirit,
Army of God, arise;
Challenge the powers of darkness,
There must be no compromise.
We shall attack their strongholds,
Our hands are trained for war;
We shall advance the kingdom,
For the victory belongs to God.

972

Dave Bilbrough.

OUR GOD IS GREAT.
(Repeat x 4)

He gave us the wind,
The sun and the snow,
The sand on the sea shore,
The flowers that grow.
Morning and evening,
Winter and spring;
Come join all creation and sing.

The gifts that He brings
Are new every day,
From glorious sunset
To soft falling rain.
The mist on the hills,
The light and the shade;
Come join all creation in praise.

For music and dancing,
The sounds that we hear;
For colours and words,
The life that we share, we say:

973

John Gibson.

OUR PASSION IS FOR YOU, Lord Jesus;
Your grace has fuelled a fire
That burns within our hearts.
There's nowhere that compares
With Your presence;
We've tasted of Your Spirit,
So there's just one thing we ask:

More, more, more, more, more.
More, more, more, more, more.
Pour out, pour out,
Pour out Your Spirit, O Lord.
Pour out, pour out,
Pour out Your Spirit, O Lord

974

Nigel Leppitt.

OVER THE HEAVENS ABOVE,
Under the earth below,
Deeper than any sea
Shines the presence of Your glory.
A river with many streams
Flows to the heart of the holy King;
Full of such wonder and mystery,
Living in power and in glory.

Great are You Lord, and mighty,
Your splendour is reigning in the earth.
Your glory is revealed
In the hearts of those who You've redeemed.
Great are You, Lord, and mighty,
Great are You, Lord, and mighty.

975

Martin Smith.

OVER THE MOUNTAINS AND THE SEA
Your river runs with love for me,
And I will open up my heart,
And let the Healer set me free.
I'm happy to be in the truth,
And I will daily lift my hands,
For I will always sing of
When Your love came down, yeah.

I could sing of Your love forever,
I could sing of Your love forever.
I could sing of Your love forever,
I could sing of Your love forever.

Oh, I feel like dancing,
It's foolishness I know;
But when the world has seen the light,
They will dance with joy
Like we're dancing now.

976

Noel Richards.

OVERWHELMED BY LOVE,
Deeper than oceans,
High as the heavens.
Ever living God
Your love has rescued me.

All my sin was laid
On Your dear Son,
Your precious One.
All my debt He paid,
Great is Your love for me.

No-one could ever earn Your love,
Your grace and mercy is free.
Lord, these words are true,
So is my love for You.

977

E. H. Bickersteth.

PEACE, PERFECT PEACE, in this dark world of sin?
The blood of Jesus whispers peace within.

Peace, perfect peace, by thronging duties pressed?
To do the will of Jesus, this is rest.

Peace, perfect peace, with sorrows surging round?
In Jesus' presence nought but calm is found.

Peace, perfect peace, with loved ones far away?
In Jesus' keeping we are safe, and they.

Peace, perfect peace, our future all unknown?
Jesus we know, and He is on the throne.

Peace, perfect peace, death shadowing us and ours?
Jesus has vanquished death and all its powers.

It is enough: earth's struggles soon shall cease,
And Jesus calls us to heaven's perfect peace.

978

Ian White.

POWER FROM ON HIGH,
Power from on high,
Lord, we are waiting
For power from on high.
Power from on high,
Power from on high,
Lord, we are waiting
For power from on high.

May we taste Your heaven
Here on the earth,
May Your Spirit bring us new birth.

May we take Your heaven
To those on the earth,
May Your Spirit bring them new birth.

May the truth and power
Of life that You give
Very soon be ours to live.

979

PRAISE AND GLORY,
Wisdom and honour,
Power and strength and thanksgiving
Be to our God forever and ever,
Amen.
(Repeat)

980

PRAISE GOD FROM WHOM ALL BLESSINGS FLOW,
Praise Him all creatures here below.
Praise Him above, you heavenly host,
Praise Father, Son and Holy Ghost.
(Repeat)

Give glory to the Father,
Give glory to the Son,
Give glory to the Spirit
While endless ages run.
'Worthy the Lamb'
All heaven cries,
'To be exalted thus:'
'Worthy the Lamb'
Our hearts reply,
'For He was slain for us.'

Praise God from whom all blessings flow,
Praise God from whom all blessings flow.
(x4)

981

Ian White.

PRAISE THE LORD,
ALL YOU SERVANTS OF THE LORD,
Who minister by night within His house.
Lift up your hands
Within the sanctuary,
And praise the Lord.

May the Lord,
The Maker of heaven and earth,
May this Lord bless you from Zion;
Lift up your hands
Within the sanctuary
And praise the Lord.

We praise You, Lord,
We praise You, Lord;
Hallelujah, we praise You, Lord.

982

David Fellingham.

PROMISE OF THE FATHER,
Given through the Son,
Of power for His children,
The Holy Spirit's come.
Young men will see visions,
Old men will dream dreams;
Sons and daughters prophesy.
Father, send Your Spirit and I'll...

Catch the fire,
As You let the power from heaven fall.
I'll catch the fire,
As Your glory falls on me.

I'll catch the fire
As I open up my life to You.
Your power will set me free.
Let Your power fall on me.

Jesus in His glory
Sends His Spirit now,
That we might be proclaimers
Of the gospel's power.
In worship and in witness
We declare God's love,
Speaking to a dying world,
Jesus has the power to save, I'll...

983 Tracy Orrison.

QUIET MY MIND, Lord,
Make me still before You;
Calm my restless heart, Lord,
Make me more like You.
(Repeat)

Raise up my hands that are hanging down;
Strengthen my feeble knees.
May Your love and joy abound,
And fill me with Your peace.

984 Luke & Nathan Fellingham.

RELEASE YOUR POWER *among us, Lord,*
That all may see Your glory.
(Repeat)

Lord, I give my life to You,
And trust Your holy name;
Help me grow in holiness,
And follow You in all Your ways.
Send Your Holy Spirit,
That I may truly be
Cleansed within my heart
And free from all impurity.

O Lord, as we come trusting our way to You,
Make our righteousness shine like the dawn.

Teach me, Lord, to listen
To the calling of Your Spirit,
Helping me and guiding me
To live my life as Jesus did.
I long to know Your power
And see the sick get healed;
Come and move among us, Lord,
That truth will be revealed.

985

Stuart Garrard.

RELEASE YOUR POWER, O GOD.

Release Your power, O God,
The visions and dreams in our hearts.
(Repeat)

Come, Holy God.
Come, Holy God.

Release Your fire, O God.
Release Your fire, O God,
A passion that burns in our hearts.
(Repeat).

986

REMEMBER YOUR CREATOR
In the days of your youth.
(Repeat 4 times)

See people old and grey,
Hear them say:
'Wish I had been that way
When I was young.
I wasn't like you, you see,
Missed the opportunity,
And now I am old
And wish I was told.'

While you are young and strong
You can sing this song,
You can serve the Lord
With all you have.
And you will have no regrets,
You have done what's best;
You have not forgot, to...

987

RIGHTEOUSNESS, PEACE, JOY IN THE HOLY GHOST;
Righteousness, peace and joy in the Holy Ghost,
That's the kingdom of God.
(Repeat)

Don't you want to be a part of the kingdom,
Don't you want to be a part of the kingdom,
Don't you want to be a part of the kingdom?
Come on, everybody!
(Repeat)

There's love in the kingdom,
So much love in the kingdom;
There's love in the kingdom.
Come on, everybody!

There's peace in the kingdom...

There's joy in the kingdom...

I'm an heir of the kingdom...

988

Peter Arajs.

RISE UP, *let Your kingdom arise in us;*
We lift our eyes to the skies, and rise up
To the brightness of His rising.
(Repeat)

All creation awaits
The revealing of the sons of God,
And all the angels of heaven
Are listening for the prayers of us:
Hearing the sound of a powerful flood,
Saints of our God who've been bought by His blood.

The redemption of God
Has given us a kingdom view,
And His promise to us,
The hope of glory, Christ in you.
Darkness shall run from the strength of His hand,
Our testimony, the blood of the Lamb.

989 Paul Oakley.

RIVER OF GOD, *flood over me,*
And lift my feet up off the ground.
Carry me out into Your sea,
And in Your presence I'll be found.

I've felt Your fire and I've felt Your rain;
And I've heard Your voice whisper my name.
I've been wading in Your river,
I've ridden on Your waves;
I've tasted of Your goodness,
Still I'm longing to be changed.

There's something inside me that just won't let go;
Why am I afraid of losing control?
Oh, I know Your love is for me,
And You'll never do me harm;
So melt away my fears,
And Holy Spirit come!

I've had enough of holding back,
I see Your goodness all around,
This time I'm opening up my heart,
So come and fill me now.

Please help me, Lord, to be more like You,
To do all the things You've called me to do.
Let me help bring in Your harvest,
Oh, I want it for Your Son;
So fill me with Your power,
Holy Spirit come!

Come like a mighty rushing wind,
A tidal wave or a monsoon rain,
Like a stream in the desert,

Or a warm summer breeze;
Gentle Dove of heaven,
Bring me to my knees!

I've had enough of holding back...

990

David Fellingham.

RUACH, Ruach,
Holy wind of God, blow on me.
Touch the fading embers, breathe on me.
Fan into a flame all that You've placed in me.
Let the fire burn more powerfully.
Ruach, Ruach,
Holy wind of God,
Holy wind of God, breathe on me.

991

Timothy Dudley-Smith.

SAFE IN THE SHADOW OF THE LORD,
Beneath His hand and power,
I trust in Him,
I trust in Him,
My fortress and my tower.

My hope is set on God alone,
Though Satan spreads his snare,
I trust in Him,
I trust in Him,
To keep me in His care.

From fears and phantoms of the night,
From foes about my way,
I trust in Him,
I trust in Him,
By darkness as by day.

His holy angels keep my feet
Secure from every stone;
I trust in Him,
I trust in Him,
And unafraid go on.

Strong in the everlasting Name,
And in my Father's care,
I trust in Him,
I trust in Him,
Who hears and answers prayer.

Safe in the shadow of the Lord,
Possessed by love divine,
I trust in Him,
I trust in Him,
And meet His love with mine.

992

Adrian Howard & Pat Turner.

SALVATION BELONGS TO OUR GOD,
Who sits on the throne,
And to the Lamb.
Praise and glory, wisdom and thanks,
Honour and power and strength:

Be to our God forever and ever,
Be to our God forever and ever,
Be to our God forever and ever, amen.

And we, the redeemed shall be strong
In purpose and unity,
Declaring aloud,
Praise and glory, wisdom and thanks,
Honour and power and strength:

993

Stuart Townend.

SAY THE WORD, I will be healed;
You are the great Physician,
You meet every need.
Say the word, I will be free;
Where chains have held me captive,
Come sing Your songs to me,
Say the word.

Say the word, I will be filled;
My hands reach out to heaven,
Where striving is stilled.
Say the word, I will be changed;
Where I am dry and thirsty,
Send cool, refreshing rain,
Say the word.

His tears have fallen like rain on my life;
Each drop a fresh revelation.
I will return to the place of the cross,
Where grace and mercy
Pour from heaven's throne.

Say the word, I will be poor,
That I might know the riches
That You have in store.
Say the word, I will be weak;
Your strength will be the power
That satisfies the meek.
Say the word.

The Lord will see the travail of His soul,
And He and I will be satisfied.
Complete the work You have started in me:
O, come Lord Jesus, shake my life again.

994

Paul Oakley.

SEARCH ME, O GOD,
And know my heart;
Know all my thoughts and my ways.
Cleanse me, O God,
Give me a pure heart,
That I may see Your face.

For You are an all consuming fire!
For You are an all consuming fire!

Teach me, O God,
Show me Your ways,
And I will walk in Your truth.
Keep me, O God,
Keep me from falling,
That I may stand before You.

Fill me, O God,
And send me out,
And I will make You known.
Give me Your heart
And Your compassion,
And let Your mercy flow.

995

Geoff Twigg.

SEND FORTH YOUR LIGHT AND YOUR TRUTH,
Let them guide me,
Let them bring me to Your holy mountain,
To the place where You dwell.
(Repeat)
(Last time)
O Lord.

Then I will come to the altar of God,
My joy and my delight;
Then I will offer the whole of my life,
A living sacrifice.

Jesus, the Way and the Truth and the Life,
My Saviour and my Lord;
Knowing Your presence will be my delight,
Your glory my reward.

996

John Pantry.

SEND ME OUT FROM HERE, *Lord,*
To serve a world in need.
May I know no man by the coat he wears,
But the heart that Jesus sees.
And may the light of Your face
Shine upon me, Lord.
You have filled my heart with the greatest joy,
And my cup is overflowing.

'Go now, and carry the news
To all creation, every race and tongue.
Take no purse with you,
Take nothing to eat
For He will supply your needs.'

'Go now, bearing the light,
Living for others,
Fearlessly walking into the night;
Take no thought for your lives,
Like lambs among wolves,
Full of the Spirit, ready to die.'

997 David Wellington.

SEND US THE RAIN, LORD,
Rain of Your Spirit,
Rain on this dry barren land.
Send us the rain, Lord,
Rain to revive us;
Cleanse us and fill us again.
Here we are, of one accord,
Calling to You, singing:
Send Your Spirit,
Send Your Spirit,
Send the rain on us again.

Pour out Your wine, Lord,
Wine of Your Spirit,
Wine that would teach us to love.
Pour out Your wine, Lord,
Oh, how we need You
To quench the thirst of our hearts.
Here we are, of one accord,
Calling to You, singing:
Send Your Spirit,
Send Your Spirit,
Pour Your wine on us again.

Breathe now upon us,
Breath of Your Spirit,
Breath to bring life to these bones.
Breathe now upon us,
Life of abundance,
Holiness, wisdom, love, truth.
Here we are, of one accord,
Calling to You, singing:
Send Your Spirit,
Send Your Spirit,
Breathe Your life on us again.

Send down the fire,
Fire of Your Spirit,
Refiner's fire to fulfil.
Send down the fire,
Fire to consume us,
Reveal Your power once more.
Here we are, of one accord,
Calling to You, singing:
Send Your Spirit,
Send Your Spirit,
Send the fire on us again.

998

Dave Bilbrough.

SEND YOUR RAIN down from the heavens;
Send Your rain to this earth.
Let there be a great outpouring;
Holy Spirit, come to us.

Send Your fire down from the heavens;
The fire of revival to Your church.
We can see the world is waiting;
Holy Spirit, come to us.

Fill this land with Your grace and mercy;
Cause our hearts to worship You.

999

Andy Park.

SHOW ME, DEAR LORD, how You see me in Your eyes,
So that I can realise Your great love for me.
Teach me, O Lord, that I am precious in Your sight,
That as a father loves his child, so You love me.

I am Yours because You have chosen me.
I'm Your child because You've called my name,
And Your steadfast love will never change;
I will always be Your precious child.

Show me, dear Lord, that I can never earn Your love,
That a gift cannot be earned, only given.
Teach me, O Lord, that Your love will never fade,
That I can never drive away Your great mercy.

1000

Matt Redman.

SHOW ME THE WAY OF THE CROSS once again,
Denying myself for the love that I've gained.
Everything's You now, everything's changed;
It's time You had my whole life,
You can have it all.

Yes, I resolve to give it all;
Some things must die, some things must live,
Not 'what can I gain', but 'what can I give'.
If much is required when much is received,
Then You can have my whole life,
Jesus, have it all.

I've given like a beggar but lived like the rich,
And crafted myself a more comfortable cross.
Yet what I am called to is deeper than this;
It's time You had my whole life,
You can have it all.

1001

David Ruis.

SING A SONG OF CELEBRATION,
Lift up a shout of praise,
For the Bridegroom will come,

The glorious One.
And oh, we will look on His face;
We'll go to a much better place.

Dance with all your might,
Lift up your hands and clap for joy:
The time's drawing near
When He will appear.
And oh, we will stand by His side;
A strong, pure, spotless Bride.

Oh, we will dance on the streets that are golden,
The glorious Bride and the great Son of Man,
From every tongue and tribe and nation
Will join in the song of the Lamb.

(Men-Women echo)
Sing aloud for the time of rejoicing is near.
The risen King, our Groom is soon to appear.
The wedding feast to come is now near at hand.
Lift up your voice, proclaim the coming Lamb.

1002

Michael Baughen.

SING TO GOD NEW SONGS of worship:
All His deeds are marvellous;
He has brought salvation to us
With His hand and holy arm:
He has shown to all the nations
Righteousness and saving power;
He recalled His truth and mercy
To His people Israel.

Sing to God new songs of worship:
Earth has seen His victory;
Let the lands of earth be joyful
Praising Him with thankfulness:

Sound upon the harp His praises,
Play to Him with melody;
Let the trumpets sound His triumph,
Show your joy to God the King!

Sing to God new songs of worship:
Let the sea now make a noise;
All on earth and in the waters
Sound your praises to the Lord:
Let the hills be joyful together,
Let the rivers clap their hands,
For with righteousness and justice
He will come to judge the earth.

1003

Stuart Garrard.

SING TO THE LORD with all of your heart;
Sing of the glory that's due to His name.
Sing to the Lord with all of your soul,
Join all of heaven and earth to proclaim:

You are the Lord, the Saviour of all,
God of creation, we praise You.
We sing the songs that awaken the dawn,
God of creation, we praise You.

Sing to the Lord with all of your mind,
With understanding give thanks to the King.
Sing to the Lord with all of your strength,
Living our lives as a praise offering.

1004

Michael Sandeman.

SOFTEN MY HEART,
That I may know
The love You have for me,
More than words or well-worn phrases.

Soften my heart,
For love to grow,
The love I have for You,
That keeps my motives pure and blameless.

Enter in,
Come and have free reign
As I walk with You today.
Risen Lamb,
Holy One,
Overshadow me today.

1005 Paul Oakley.

SOMETIMES WHEN I FEEL YOUR LOVE

As I walk along the busy street,
I whisper Your name under my breath.
And sometimes when I feel Your touch
In the quiet place of my room,
I sing Your name in adoration.
And there are times when I feel like I'm bursting
With Your love so strong and so true;
And in my heart I feel such a yearning,
And I want all the world
To know You love them, too.

I love Your love,
Gonna shout it out aloud.
I love Your love,
Wanna tell the world about it.
I love Your love,
'Cause I've found it to be true,
And I live to love You, too.

1006

Paul Oakley.

SON OF MAN and Man of heaven,
Full of grace and truth;
Sinner's friend yet without sin,
I want to be like You:
Perfect in holiness,
Full of faithfulness and love.

I want to be like Jesus,
I want to be like Jesus,
I want to be like You,
O Lord, our God.
(Repeat)

You began a work in me,
I know You'll see it through.
There's a new song in my heart,
And I want to sing to You.
You lifted me from mire,
From sin and from shame You set me free,
And I know Your tenderness,
I know Your power at work in me.

You're making me like Jesus ...

1007

Andrae Crouch.

SOON, AND VERY SOON,
We are going to see the King;
Soon, and very soon,
We are going to see the King;
Soon, and very soon,
We are going to see the King;
Alleluia, alleluia,
We're going to see the King!

No more crying there ...

No more dying there ...

Alleluia, alleluia,
Alleluia, alleluia.

Soon, and very soon ...

Alleluia ...

1008 Dave Bilbrough.

SOUND THE TRUMPET, strike the drum,
See the King of glory come,
Join the praises rising from
The people of the Lord.
Let your voices now be heard,
Unrestrained and unreserved,
Prepare the way for His return,
You people of the Lord.

Sing Jesus is Lord;
Jesus is Lord.

Bow down to His authority,
For He has slain the enemy.
Of heaven and hell He holds the key.
Jesus is Lord;
Jesus is Lord.

1009 Chris Bowater.

SPIRIT OF GOD, SHOW ME JESUS,
Remove the darkness,
Let truth shine through!
Spirit of God, show me Jesus,
Reveal the fulness of His love to me.

1010

SPIRIT OF HOLINESS,
Wisdom and faithfulness,
Wind of the Lord,
Blowing strongly and free:
Strength of our serving
And joy of our worshipping;
Spirit of God,
Bring Your fulness to me!

You came to interpret
And teach us effectively
All that the Saviour
Has spoken and done;
To glorify Jesus is all Your activity;
Promise and Gift
Of the Father and Son:

You came with Your gifts
To supply all our poverty,
Pouring Your love
On the church in her need;
You came with Your fruit
For our growth to maturity,
Richly refreshing
The souls that You feed:

1011

STANDING IN YOUR PRESENCE,
Lord, my heart and life are changed;
Just to love You and to live to
See Your beauty and Your grace.

Heaven and earth cry out Your name,
Nations rise up and see Your face;
And Your kingdom is established
As I live to know You more.
Now I will never be the same;
Spirit of God, my life You've changed,
And I'll forever sing Your praise.
I live to know You, Lord.
I live to know You, Lord.

You've called me, I will follow;
Your will for me I'm sure.
Let Your heartbeat be my heart's cry,
Let me live to serve Your call.

1012 Dave Browning.

TAKE ME PAST THE OUTER COURTS,
And through the holy place,
Past the brazen altar,
Lord, I want to see Your face.
Pass me by the crowds of people,
And the priests who sing their praise;
I hunger and thirst for Your righteousness,
But it's only found one place,

So take me into the Holy of holies,
Take me in by the blood of the Lamb;
So take me into the Holy of holies,
Take the coal, cleanse my lips, here I am.

1013 Graham Kendrick & Steve Thompson.

TEACH ME TO DANCE *to the beat of Your heart,*
Teach me to move in the power of Your Spirit,
Teach me to walk in the light of Your presence,
Teach me to dance to the beat of Your heart.

Teach me to love with Your heart of compassion,
Teach me to trust in the word of Your promise,
Teach me to hope in the day of Your coming,
Teach me to dance to the beat of Your heart.

You wrote the rhythm of life,
Created heaven and earth;
In You is joy without measure.
So, like a child in Your sight,
I dance to see Your delight,
For I was made for Your pleasure,
Pleasure.

Let all my movements express
A heart that loves to say 'yes',
A will that leaps to obey You.
Let all my energy blaze
To see the joy in Your face;
Let my whole being praise You,
Praise You.

1014

Kevin Prosch.

TEACH US, O LORD, what it really means
To rend our hearts instead of outer things.
And teach us, O God, what we do not see
About our hearts and of Your ways.
And Father deal with our carnal desires,
To move in Your power, but not live the life,
And to love our neighbour with all that we have,
And keep our tongues from saying things we have not seen.

O, break our hearts with the things that break Yours,
If we sow in tears, we will reap in joy,
That we might pass through Your refining fire,
Where brokenness awaits on the other side.

Raise up an army like Joel saw,
Your church that is stronger than ever before.
They do not break ranks when they plunge through
defences,
But the fear of the Lord will be their wisdom.
That they might weep as Jesus wept,
A fountain of tears for the wounded and lost;
Whoever heard of an army, O God,
That conquered the earth by weeping,
And mourning, and brokenness?

But there will be a day when the nations will bow
And our Lord will be King over all the earth;
And He will be the only One,
And also His name will be the only One.

1015

Martin Smith.

THANK YOU FOR SAVING ME;
What can I say?
You are my everything,
I will sing Your praise.
You shed Your blood for me;
What can I say?
You took my sin and shame,
A sinner called by name.

Great is the Lord.
Great is the Lord.
For we know Your truth has set us free;
You've set Your hope in me.

Mercy and grace are mine,
Forgiven is my sin;
Jesus, my only hope,
The Saviour of the world.

'Great is the Lord,' we cry;
God, let Your kingdom come.
Your word has let me see,
Thank You for saving me.

1016

Richard Lewis.

THE ANGELS AROUND YOUR THRONE,
They cry, 'Holy is the Lamb.'
The angels around Your throne,
They cry, 'Holy is the Lamb.'
So we sing holy, holy, holy,
Holy is the Lamb.
So we sing holy, holy, holy,
Holy is the Lamb.

The angels around Your throne,
They cry, 'Worthy is the Lamb.'
The angels around Your throne,
They cry, 'Worthy is the Lamb.'
So we sing worthy, worthy, worthy,
Worthy is the Lamb.
So we sing worthy, worthy, worthy,
Worthy is the Lamb.

1017

Matt Redman.

THE ANGELS, LORD, THEY SING
Around Your throne;
And we will join their song:
Praise You alone.
(Repeat)

Holy, holy, holy,
Lord our God,
Who was and is and is to come.
(Repeat)

The living creatures, Lord,
Speak endless praise;
And joining at Your throne,
We'll sing their sweet refrain.
(Repeat)

The elders, Lord, they fall
Before Your throne;
Our hearts we humbly bow
To You alone.
(Repeat)

1018

Doug Horley.

THE BATTLE IS THE LORD'S,
The battle is the Lord's,
The battle is the Lord's
That is our victory cry.
(Repeat)

We refuse to bow to satan's schemes,
Set our wills for righteousness;
We declare we'll choose for truth
In every situation.
We could battle in the heavenlies,
Yet in our lives neglect to fight:
Saying no to self and no to sin
Is where our warfare must begin.

As we're taking ground in daily war,
Living lives of righteousness,
We will grow in strength to face
The bigger situations.
And the more of us that battle through,
The purer then this church will be;
Who will stop us then as we proclaim:
'Strongholds, you have had your day!'

1019

Matt Redman & Martin Smith.

THE CROSS HAS SAID IT ALL,
The cross has said it all.
I can't deny what You have shown,
The cross speaks of a God of love;
There displayed for all to see,
Jesus Christ, our only hope,
A message of the Father's heart:
'Come, my children, come on home.'

As high as the heavens are above the earth,
So high is the measure of Your great love;
As far as the east is from the west,
So far have You taken our sins from us.
(Repeat)

The cross has said it all,
The cross has said it all.
I never recognised Your touch
Until I met You at the cross;
We are fallen, dust to dust,
How could You do this for us?
Son of God shed precious blood:
Who can comprehend this love?

How high, how wide, how deep; *(Repeat x4)*
How high!

1020

Martin Smith.

THE CRUCIBLE FOR SILVER
And the furnace for gold,
But the Lord tests the heart of this child.
Standing in all purity,
God, our passion is for holiness,
Lead us to the secret place of praise.

Jesus, Holy One,
You are my heart's desire.
King of kings, my everything,
You've set this heart on fire.
(Repeat)

Father, take our offering, with our song we humbly praise
You.
You have brought Your holy fire to our lips.
Standing in Your beauty, Lord,
Your gift to us is holiness;
Lead us to the place where we can sing:

1021

Dave Bilbrough & Andy Piercy.

THE DAY OF THE STREAMS *is over,*
The time of the river is here.
(Repeat x4)

I hear the sound of a mighty river,
Of rushing water running free
To every land, through every border,
Flowing now across this earth.

There is a time I know is coming,
When all God's people join as one;
They will become a great awakening,
Bringing life to all the world.

And the river is flowing,
Getting wider and wider,
Deeper and deeper
As it flows from the throne;
And the leaves on the trees
Are for the healing of the nations,
It's as clear as crystal,
It's the water of life.

1022

THE EARTH RESOUNDS IN SONGS OF PRAISE;
Creation shouts Your glorious name,
And the skies speak forth Your majesty,
And the heavens declare Your glory.
Your kingdom rules from age to age;
Every tribe and tongue shall bring You praise,
And we come to bow before the throne
Of the Lord of the heavens and earth.

Jesus, King of kings,
Jesus, Lord of lords,
We proclaim Your kingdom come,
Jesus, Son of God.
Lord, enthroned on high
Above the heavens and the earth,
We proclaim Your kingdom come!

1023

THE GRACE OF GOD upon my life
Is not dependent upon me,
On what I have done
Or deserved,
But a gift of mercy from God
Which has been given unto me
Because of His love,
His love for me.

It is unending, unfailing,
Unlimited, unmerited,
The grace of God given unto me.
It is unending, unfailing,
Unlimited, unmerited,
The grace of God given unto me.

1024 Lex Loizides.

THE HEAVENS THEY PREACH, they preach,
They preach the glorious splendour of God.
The stars in the sky seem so out of reach,
Yet they whisper His wonderful love.
Day after day in a sermon of nature
The works of His hands lift their voice:
'Wake up, you nations, and serve Your Creator,
There's mercy in Him, so rejoice!'

And I'll lift my heart and my hands to Him,
And I'll let my life shine with love
To God's wonderful Son.
He wears the crown, He's the King.
Come and behold Him now,
Come and delight in His excellent virtues;
Seek Him while He can be found,
For He is the help and the hope
For all the world.

The prophets, they preached, they preached,
They preached that one day a Saviour would come;
And suddenly men heard a heavenly speech,
The voice of God's only Son.
Day after day in the streets and the temple
He taught them and met their needs,
And now through His death and His great resurrection
His glorious purpose succeeds.

Your people will preach, we'll preach,
We'll preach the unfailing riches of Christ;
There's no one who's fallen too far from His reach,
Who can't come from death into life.
Day after day at the dawn of revival
The multitudes seek His face,
As we work to speed on His final arrival
And crown Him with glory and praise!

1025 Stuart Townend & Kevin Jamieson.

THE KING OF LOVE is my delight,
His eyes are fire, His face is light,
The First and Last, the Living One,
His name is Jesus.
And from His mouth there comes a sound
That shakes the earth and splits the ground,
And yet this voice is life to me,
The voice of Jesus.

And I will sing my songs of love,
Calling out across the earth;
The King has come,
The King of love has come.
And troubled minds can know His peace,
Captive hearts can be released;
The King has come,
The King of love has come.

My Lover's breath is sweetest wine,
I am His prize, and He is mine;
How can a sinner know such joy?
Because of Jesus.
The wounds of love are in His hands,
The price is paid for sinful man;
Accepted child, forgiven son,
Because of Jesus.

And my desire is to have You near;
Lord, You know that You are welcome here.
Before such love, before such grace
I will let the walls come down.

1026

Donald Fishel.

THE LIGHT OF CHRIST
Has come into the world;
The light of Christ
Has come into the world.

All men must be born again
To see the kingdom of God;
The water and the Spirit
Bring new life in God's love.

God gave up His only Son
Out of love for the world,
So that all men who believe in Him
Will live forever.

The light of God has come to us
So that we might have salvation;
From the darkness of our sins we walk
Into glory with Christ Jesus.

1027

Merrilyn Billing.

THE LORD FILLS ME WITH HIS STRENGTH,
And protects me wherever I go.
The Lord fills me with His strength,
And protects me wherever I go.

Wherever I go, wherever I go,
The Lord protects me wherever I go.
Wherever I go, wherever I go,
The Lord protects me wherever I go.

1028

Paul Oakley.

THE LORD HAS SPOKEN. *(Men/Women echo)*
His purpose stands. *(Men/Women echo)*
The Lord has spoken. *(Men/Women echo)*
His purpose stands. *(Men/Women echo)*

Does God speak and then not act?
Make a vow and not fulfil?
I will choose to serve the Lord
Wholeheartedly, wholeheartedly.

(Ch 1.)
Oh, raise up a church
With a different spirit,
Like Caleb's spirit, believing Your word.
Oh, raise up a church who will not sin,
They press on in to possess the land.

You began with just one man,
A covenant with Abraham,
Promising that through his seed
The nations would be blessed,
And now Your plan is manifest.

(Repeat Ch1.)

(Ch2.)
Oh, raise up a church who walk by faith,
In the fear of God they overcome.
Oh, raise up a church
Whose God is with them,
They walk in wisdom, they fear no harm.

Deliver us from the fear of man,
And by Your grace we shall stand.
We'll call to mind Your mighty works
And Your acts of sovereign power;
We'll gather strength as we agree
The battle belongs to the Lord.

(Repeat Ch1. & Ch2.)

(Ch 3.)
Oh, raise up a church
Who revere Your judgements,
They lift up a banner of mercy and love.
Oh, raise up a church
Who'll not keep silent,
They speak of the glory of Your dear Son.

1029

Daniel C Stradwick.

THE LORD REIGNS, *the Lord reigns,*
The Lord reigns,
Let the earth rejoice, let the earth rejoice,
Let the earth rejoice.
Let the people be glad
That our God reigns.

A fire goes before Him
And burns up all His enemies;
The hills melt like wax
At the presence of the Lord,
At the presence of the Lord.

The heavens declare His righteousness,
The peoples see His glory;
For You, O Lord, are exalted
Over all the earth,
Over all the earth.

1030

Stuart Townend.

THE LORD'S MY SHEPHERD, I'll not want.
He makes me lie in pastures green.
He leads me by the still, still waters,
His goodness restores my soul.

And I will trust in You alone.
And I will trust in You alone,
For Your endless mercy follows me,
Your goodness will lead me home.

(Descant)
I will trust, I will trust in You.
I will trust, I will trust in You.
Endless mercy follows me,
Goodness will lead me home.

He guides my ways in righteousness,
And He anoints my head with oil,
And my cup, it overflows with joy,
I feast on His pure delights.

And though I walk the darkest path,
I will not fear the evil one,
For You are with me, and Your rod and staff
Are the comfort I need to know.

1031

Geoff Bullock.

THE LOVE OF GOD, heaven's hope;
This perfect peace, this rest for my soul.
This love divine, portrayed in pain,
The cross stands alone,
Unfailing love.

This love of God, creation's cry;
Perfection portrayed, broken for me.
The Author of life has suffered our pain.
The cross stands alone,
Unfailing love.

The love of God was found in the nails;
The love of God was seen in the scars.
The light and the life was darkened by death,
My hope and salvation carried to life,
Unfailing love.

The love of God, written in blood;
This empty grave, the stone rolled away!
The mercy of God has triumphed in Christ.
The cross stands alone,
Unfailing love.

1032

Louise Hunt & Nathan Fellingham.

THE NAME OF THE LORD is a strong tower;
The name of the Lord brings refuge and strength.
The name of the Lord gives hope to the hopeless;
The name of the Lord breathes life to the dead.

The name of the Lord give strength to the weary,
The name of the Lord brings freedom from fear;
The name of the Lord gives peace to the restless,
The name of the Lord will heal the oppressed.

O Lord, You never change,
Holy God, You remain the same,
For Your love, it never fades,
Your faithfulness surrounds me.

For You alone are God, and I bow before You.
You alone are God, I worship, adore You.
You alone are God, none other before You,
And I offer up my life again.

The name of the Lord covers me with mercy,
The name of the Lord brings everlasting joy;
The name of the Lord will lift all my burdens,
The name of the Lord, it makes me complete.

I call, and You answer me,
For You know my every need.
In Your love I put my trust,
Your faithfulness surrounds me.

O taste and see
That the Lord is good.
How blessèd is the man
Who hides himself in Him.

1033

Stuart Townend.

THERE IS A HOME that wanderers seek,
There is a strength that lifts the weak;
There is hope for those that know despair.
There is a cup that satisfies,
There is a Friend who dries my eyes;
There is peace for those with heavy hearts.

Tender mercy,
The tender mercy of our God,
From lips of sinners
He has heard the faintest cry.
Tender mercy,
The tender mercy of our God,
He has relented and His grace is my delight.

I have resolved to know Him more,
He whom the hosts of heaven adore,
Mighty King, whose reign will never end.
Yet as I gaze at the Holy One,
He beckons me to closer come,
Bares the scars that show to me my worth.

1034

Matt Redman.

THERE IS A LOUDER SHOUT TO COME,
There is a sweeter song to hear;
All the nations with one voice,
All the people with one fear.
Bowing down before Your throne,
Every tribe and tongue will be;
All the nations with one voice,
All the people with one King.
And what a song we'll sing upon that day.

O what a song we'll sing and
O what a tune we'll bear;
You deserve an anthem of the highest praise.
O what a joy will rise and
O what a sound we'll make;
You deserve an anthem of the highest praise.

Now we see a part of this,
One day we shall see in full;
All the nations with one voice,
All the people with one love.
No one else will share Your praise,
Nothing else can take Your place;
All the nations with one voice,
All the people with one Lord.
And what a song we'll sing upon that day.

Even now upon the earth
There's a glimpse of all to come;
Many people with one voice,
Harmony of many tongues.
We will all confess Your name,
You will be our only praise;
All the nations with one voice,
All the people with one God.
And what a song we'll sing upon that day.

1035 Lenny LeBlanc.

THERE IS NONE LIKE YOU,
No one else can touch my heart like You do.
I could search for all eternity long and find
There is none like You.

Your mercy flows like a river wide,
And healing comes from Your hands.
Suffering children are safe in Your arms;
There is none like You.

1036 Noel & Tricia Richards.

THERE IS NO ONE LIKE OUR GOD *in all the earth.*
There is no one like our God in all the earth.
No one like our God,
No one like our God.

Our God has made the heavens,
Our God has made the earth;
And everything that lives,
His word has brought to birth.

He numbers every star,
And calls each one by name;
He fills the skies with clouds,
Supplies the earth with rain.

Sing praises to our God,
Sing praises to His name;
His love will never end,
His word will never fail.

God is with us.
God is with us.
God is with us.

1037

David Ruis.

THERE IS NO OTHER FRIEND,
There is no other friend like You, O Lord;
No other brother, no other sister like You.
There is no other love,
There is no other love like You, O Lord;
No other sweeter, no other fountain but You.

How long until I'm satisfied?
I must have more of You.
For I was born in Zion,
Awakened love is crying out for You.
Lord, it must be You!

If I am healed by just one touch of Your garment, Lord,
Then how much more of Your love is for me
Than I'm tasting, Lord?
Draw me, take me, I will run
Over the mountains and down
Into the valley, I will run with You.

Ah, all my fountains are in You.
(Repeat)

1038

Robert Critchley.

THERE IS ONE NAME under heaven
By which men can be saved,
Jesus alone.
Only one name under heaven,
Jesus, and Jesus alone.

One sacrifice,
One holy Lamb
Shed His own blood,
Paid for my sin;

And this righteous One,
God's only Son,
I sing my praises to Him,
I sing my praises to Him.

1039

Geoff Bullock.

THERE'S A LIGHT THAT SHINES, a lamp that burns,
The hope, the peace of righteousness.
And You who hear the prayers of all,
You call us near to You.

There's a path that leads, a way that's true,
The life, the light, the perfect truth.
We come to You forgiven, free,
You call us near to You.

And the light shines so we can see,
And the truth came so we could know.
And the light of God is the light of men,
And His life gives life to all.

No other way, no other life,
No other truth, no other light.
The way ahead is found in Christ,
You call us near to You.

We will dance and sing, for freedom comes
To heal our hearts and dry our tears.
Forever more in glorious light
You call us near to You.

1040

Richard Lewis.

THERE'S AN AWESOME SOUND
On the winds of heaven,
Mighty thunder clouds
In the skies above.
The immortal King,
Who will reign forever,
Is reaching out with His arms of love,
His arms of love,
His arms of love.

All creation sings
Of the Lamb of glory,
Who laid down His life
For all the world.
What amazing love,
That the King of heaven
Should be crucified,
Stretching out His arms,
His arms of love,
His arms of love.

Send revival to this land,
Fill this nation with Your love.
(Repeat)

1041

Paul Oakley.

THERE'S A PLACE WHERE THE STREETS SHINE
With the glory of the Lamb.
There's a way, we can go there,
We can live there beyond time.

Because of You, because of You,
Because of Your love,
Because of Your blood.

No more pain, no more sadness,
No more suffering, no more tears.
No more sin, no more sickness,
No injustice, no more death.

Because of You, because of You,
Because of Your love,
Because of Your blood.

All our sins are washed away,
And we can live forever,
Now we have this hope,
Because of You.
Oh, we'll see You face to face,
And we will dance together
In the city of our God,
Because of You.

There is joy everlasting,
There is gladness, there is peace.
There is wine ever flowing,
There's a wedding, there's a feast.

1042

Malcolm du Plessis.

THERE'S A RIVER flowing from the throne,
Not a gentle stream but powerful flow.
It brings the city of our God such joy,
And springs up fountains in her midst.
On the banks the trees are full of life,
The fruit just grows and grows all the year round.
The leaves are green and never seem to die,
They're for the healing of this world.

There's a river, there's a river,
There's a river flowing from the throne.
There's a river, there's a river
And it flows through out the world.

There's a river, there's a river,
There's a river flowing from the throne.
There's a river, there's a river
And it's flooding over me.

You invited me to come for free,
Enjoy the feast You had prepared for me;
Draw with laughter from Your sparkling wells,
Bathe in Your river of delights.
First You led me to the edge of the stream,
Cautiously I put my ankles in;
The thrill was just too much to describe,
And I heard You call me deeper still!

1043

Taran Ash, James Mott & Matthew Pryce.

THERE'S A RIVER OF JOY that flows from Your
throne,
O river of joy flow through me.
There's a river of joy that flows from Your throne:
Come, Holy Spirit, with joy,
Come, Holy Spirit, with joy.

I will rise up on the wings of an eagle;
With joy I receive Your love.
I will praise You with a song everlasting.
Thank You, Lord, for Your love.
Thank You, Lord, for Your love.

1044

David Ruis.

THERE'S A WIND A-BLOWING
All across the land;
Fragrant breeze of heaven
Blowing once again.
Don't know where it comes from,

Don't know where it goes,
But let it blow over me.
Oh, sweet wind,
Come and blow over me.

There's a rain a-pouring,
Showers from above;
Mercy drops are coming,
Mercy drops of love.
Turn your face to heaven,
Let the water pour,
Well, let it pour over me.
Oh, sweet rain,
Come and pour over me.

There's a fire burning,
Falling from the sky;
Awesome tongues of fire,
Consuming you and I.
Can you feel it burning,
Burn the sacrifice?
Well, let it burn over me.
Oh, sweet fire,
Come and burn over me.

1045

Eddie Espinosa

THERE'S NO ONE LIKE YOU, my Lord,
No one could take Your place;
My heart beats to worship You,
I live just to seek Your face.
There's no one like You, my Lord,
No one could take Your place;
There's no one like You, my Lord,
No one like You.

You are my God,
You're everything to me;
There's no one like You, my Lord,
No one like You.
You are my God.
You're everything to me;
There's no one like You, my Lord,
No one like You.

There's no one like You, my Lord,
No one could take Your place;
I long for Your presence, Lord,
To serve You is my reward.
There's no one like You, my Lord,
No one could take Your place;
There's no one like You, my Lord,
No one like You.

1046

Ian Smale.

THERE'S NOTHING I LIKE BETTER THAN TO PRAISE.

There's nothing I like better
Than to praise.
'Cause Lord, I love You,
And there's nothing I would rather do
Than whisper about it,
Talk all about it.
Shout all about it all my days.

1047

Robin Mark.

THESE ARE THE DAYS OF ELIJAH,
Declaring the word of the Lord:
And these are the days of Your servant Moses,
Righteousness being restored.

And though these are days of great trial,
Of famine and darkness and sword,
Still, we are a voice in the desert crying
'Prepare ye the way of the Lord.'

Behold He comes riding on the clouds,
Shining like the sun at the trumpet call;
Lift your voice, it's the year of jubilee,
Out of Zion's hill salvation comes.

These are the days of Ezekiel,
The dry bones becoming as flesh;
And these are the days of Your servant David,
Rebuilding the temple of praise.
These are the days of the harvest,
The fields are as white in the world,
And we are the labourers in the vineyard,
Declaring the word of the Lord.

1048

Mick Gisbey.

THE SKY IS FILLED with the glory of God.
Triumphantly the angels sing:
'Rejoice, good news, a Saviour is born,
And life will never be the same.'

Emmanuel.
Emmanuel.
Emmanuel.

Praise and adoration spring from our hearts,
We lift our voices unto You;
You are the One, God's only Son,
King of kings forever more!

1049

Andy Park.

THE SPIRIT OF THE SOVEREIGN LORD is upon you,
Because He has anointed you
To preach good news.
(Repeat)

He has sent you to the poor, *(Men)*
This is the year: *(Women)*
To bind up the brokenhearted, *(Men)*
This is the day: *(Women)*
To bring freedom to the captives, *(Men)*
This is the year: *(Women)*
And to release the ones in darkness. *(All)*

This is the year of the favour of the Lord.
This is the day of the vengeance of our God.
This is the year of the favour of the Lord.
This is the day of the vengeance of our God.

The Spirit of the Sovereign Lord is upon us,
Because He has anointed us
To preach good news.
(Repeat)

He will comfort all who mourn *(Men)*
This is the year: *(Women)*
He will provide for those who grieve; *(Men)*
This is the day: *(Women)*
He will pour out the oil of gladness, *(Men)*
This is the year: *(Women)*
Instead of mourning you will praise. *(All)*

1050

Author unknown.

THE VIRGIN MARY HAD A BABY BOY,
The Virgin Mary had a baby boy,
The Virgin Mary had a baby boy,
And they said that His name was Jesus.

He come from the glory,
He come from the glorious kingdom.
He come from the glory,
He come from the glorious kingdom.
Oh, yes! believer.
Oh, yes! believer.
He come from the glory,
He come from the glorious kingdom.

The angels sang when the baby was born,
The angels sang when the baby was born,
The angels sang when the baby was born,
And proclaiming Him the Saviour Jesus.

The wise men saw where the baby was born,
The wise men saw where the baby was born,
The wise men saw where the baby was born,
And they saw that His name was Jesus.

1051

Dave Bilbrough.

THE WAVES ARE BREAKING, the tide is turning,
God's Spirit is coming to this earth;
The harvest is waiting,
And we have been called
To go to the nations of this world.

To the ends of the earth,
To the ends of the earth,
To the ends of the earth we will go;
Bearing the message
That our God can be known,
To the ends of the earth we will go.

The fire is falling, the wind is blowing,
The flame is spreading across our land;
Revival is coming, let the world hear,
Tell every woman, child and man.

The drums are beating,
The trumpet is sounding,
A warrior spirit He's put in our hearts;
In the name of the Father, Spirit and Son,
We'll take this word to everyone.

1052 Noel & Tricia Richards.

THE WORLD IS LOOKING FOR A HERO;
We know the greatest One of all:
The mighty Ruler of the nations,
King of kings and Lord of lords;
Who took the nature of a servant,
And gave His life to save us all.

We will raise a shout,
We will shout it out,
He is the Champion of the world.
(Repeat)

The Lord Almighty is our hero,
He breaks the stranglehold of sin.
Through Jesus' love we fear no evil;
Powers of darkness flee from Him.
His light will shine in every nation,
A sword of justice He will bring.

1053 Kevin Prosch.

THEY THAT WAIT ON THE LORD
Will renew their strength,
Run and not get weary,
Walk and not faint.
(Repeat)

Do you not know?
Have you not heard?
My Father does not get weary.
He'll give passion to a willing heart:
Even the youths get tired and faint,
But strength will come for those who wait.

If you wait on the Lord
You'll renew your strength,
Run and not get weary,
Walk and not faint.
(Repeat)

I will wait, I will wait, I will wait on You;
I will run, I will run, I will run with You;
My love, my love, my love for You.

1054

Christopher Idle.

THIS EARTH BELONGS TO GOD,
The world, its wealth, and all its people;
He formed the waters wide
And fashioned every sea and shore.
Who may go up the hill of the Lord
And stand in the place of holiness?
Only the one whose heart is pure,
Whose hands and lips are clean.

Lift high your heads, you gates,
Rise up, you everlasting doors,
As here now the King of glory
Enters into full command.
Who is the King, this King of glory?
Where is the throne He comes to claim?
Christ is the King, the Lord of glory,
Fresh from His victory.

Lift high your heads, you gates,
And fling wide open the ancient doors,
For here the King of glory
Takes universal power.
Who is this king, this King of glory,
What is the power by which He reigns?
Christ is the King, His cross of glory,
And by love He rules.

All glory be to God
The Father, Son and Holy Spirit;
From ages past it was,
Is now, and ever more shall be.

1055

Kent Henry & David Ortinau.

THIS GOD IS OUR GOD,
God of power, God of might.
This God is our God,
God of wisdom and light.
(Repeat)

And we meditate on Your great love,
Your praises fill the earth.
The villages of Judah shout
That you will be, forever be
Our guide unto the end.

As we have heard, so we have seen
The safety of our God,
That we might tell all generations
You will be, forever be
Our guide unto the end.

1056

Mark Altrogge.

THIS I KNOW, *my God is for me,*
This I know.
This I know, my God is on my side;
My God is for me, this I know.

If God did not spare His only Son,
But delivered Him up for us all,
Will He not give us every good thing
When we come in His name and call?

Let us draw near the throne of grace
For mercy and help in our need;
For Jesus is ever praying for us,
He is living to intercede.

1057

Christopher Beatty.

THIS IS HOLY GROUND,
We're standing on holy ground,
For the Lord is here
And where He is holy.
This is holy ground,
We're standing on holy ground,
For the Lord is here
And where He is holy.

These are holy hands,
He's given us holy hands,
He works through these hands
And so these hands are holy.
These are holy hands,
He's given us holy hands,
He works through these hands
And so these hands are holy.

1058 Graham Kendrick.

THIS IS MY BELOVÈD SON
Who tasted death
That you, my child, might live.
See the blood He shed for you,
What suffering!
Say what more could He give?
Clothed in His perfection,
Bring praise, a fragrance sweet,
Garlanded with joy,
Come worship at His feet:

That the Lamb who was slain
Might receive the reward,
Might receive the reward of His suffering.

Look, the world's great harvest fields
Are ready now,
And Christ commands us: 'Go!'
Countless souls are dying
So hopelessly,
His wondrous love unknown.
Lord, give us the nations
For the glory of the King.
Father, send more labourers,
The lost to gather in.

Come the day when we will stand
There face to face,
What joy will fill His eyes.
For at last His Bride appears,
So beautiful,
Her glory fills the skies.
Drawn from every nation,
People, tribe and tongue;
All creation sings,
The wedding has begun.

And the Lamb who was slain
Shall receive the reward,
Shall receive the reward of His suffering.

1059

Sue Rinaldi.

THIS IS MY PILGRIMAGE,
To climb into You.
This is my pilgrimage,
To be absorbed by You.

I'm so restless for more of You, O God.
I'm so restless, hear these words, O God.

Give me the eyes of a prophet,
Help me to see the unseen,
I long to hear the music of heaven,
As the angels play in my ears.
Sometimes I'm war torn and weary,
Sometimes I'm willing and strong,
But at this moment I'm standing before You
As Your restless pilgrim.

I'll fix my eyes on You,
I'll tread the path with You,
I'll be a warrior of love for You.

But I'm so restless . . .

1060

Chris Bowater & Phil Lawson Johnston.

THIS IS THE MYSTERY,
That Christ has chosen you and me
To be the revelation of His glory;
A chosen, royal, holy people,
Set apart and loved,
A Bride preparing for her King.

Let the Bride say 'come',
Let the Bride say 'come',
Let the Bride of the Lamb
Say 'come, Lord Jesus!'
Let the Bride say 'come',
Let the Bride say 'come',
Let the Bride of the Lamb
Say 'come, Lord Jesus, come!'

She's crowned in splendour
And a royal diadem,
The King is enthralled by her beauty.
Adorned in righteousness,
Arrayed in glorious light,
The Bride in waiting for her King.

Now hear the Bridegroom call,
'Beloved, come aside;
The time of betrothal is at hand.
Lift up your eyes and see
The dawning of the day,
When as King, I'll return to claim My Bride.'

1061

Dave Bilbrough.

THIS IS THE PLACE
Where dreams are found,
Where vision comes,
Called holy ground.

Holy ground,
I'm standing on holy ground,
For the Lord my God
Is here with me.

Your fire burns
But never dies;
I realise
This is holy ground.

The Great I AM,
Revealed to man;
Take off your shoes,
This is holy ground.

1062 Geoff Bullock.

THIS LOVE, this hope,
This peace of God, this righteousness,
This faith, this joy,
This life complete in me.

Now healed and whole,
And risen in His righteousness,
I live in Him,
He lives in me,
And filled with this hope in God,
Reflecting His glory.

Now is the time to worship You,
Now is the time to offer You
All of my thoughts, my dreams and plans;
I lay it down.
Now is the time to live for You,
Now is the time I'm found in You.
Now is the time Your kingdom comes.

1063 Ian White.

THOUGH I FEEL AFRAID
Of territory unknown,
I know that I can say
That I do not stand alone.
For Jesus, You have promised
Your presence in my heart;
I cannot see the ending,
But it's here that I must start.

And all I know is You have called me,
And that I will follow is all I can say.
I will go where You will send me,
And Your fire lights my way.

What lies across the waves
May cause my heart to fear;
Will I survive the day,
Must I leave what's known and dear?
A ship that's in the harbour
Is still and safe from harm,
But it was not built to be there,
It was made for wind and storm.

1064 James Wright.

THROUGHOUT THE EARTH YOUR GLORY WILL COME,
A day of power, of salvation.
To thirsty hearts Your rivers will run,
Changing lives for the glory of God.
From Satan's hold this land will be free,
The deaf will hear, the blind will see;
To walk in truth, in victory,
To live for the glory of God.

Lord, come and reign by the power of Your Spirit,
Shower this land with Your rivers of life,
That Jesus the Son would be glorified
Within the heart of Your Bride,
Lord, come and reign.

Upon the earth may Your kingdom come,
Within our lives may Your will be done;
Under the reign of Jesus the Son
We will live for the glory of God.
The gates of heaven are open wide,
To bless this land, to turn back the tide,
To welcome in Your glorious Bride,
To live for the glory of God.

1065 Edward Hayes Plumptre.

THY HAND, O GOD HAS GUIDED
Thy flock, from age to age;
The wondrous tale is written,
Full clear on every page.
Our fathers owned Thy goodness,
And we their deeds record;
And both of this bear witness:
One Church, one Faith, one Lord.

Thy heralds brought glad tidings
To greatest as to least;
They bade them rise and hasten
To share the great King's feast.
And this was all their teaching
In every deed and word;
To all alike proclaiming:
One Church, one Faith, one Lord.

Through many a day of darkness,
Through many a scene of strife,
The faithful few fought bravely
To guard the nation's life.
Their gospel of redemption,
Sin pardoned, man restored,
Was all in this enfolded:
One Church, one Faith, one Lord.

Thy mercy will not fail us,
Nor leave Thy work undone;
With Thy right hand to help us,
The victory shall be won.
And then, by men and angels,
Thy name shall be adored,
And this shall be their anthem:
One Church, one Faith, one Lord.

1066

Amy Grant & Michael W. Smith.

THY WORD *is a lamp unto my feet*
And a light unto my path.
(Repeat)

When I feel afraid,
Think I've lost my way,
Still You're there right beside me.
And nothing will I fear
As long as You are near;
Please be near me to the end.

I will not forget
Your love for me, and yet
My heart forever is wandering.
Jesus, be my guide
And hold me to Your side,
And I will love You to the end.

1067

Noel Richards.

TO BE IN YOUR PRESENCE,
To sit at Your feet,
Where Your love surrounds me,
And makes me complete.

This is my desire, O Lord,
This is my desire.
This is my desire, O Lord,
This is my desire.

To rest in Your presence,
Not rushing away;
To cherish each moment,
Here I would stay.

1068

TO HIM WHO LOVES US,
And has freed us from our sins
By His blood,
And has made us to be a kingdom
And priests to serve His God.
(Repeat)
And Father.

(Men-Women echo each line)
To Him be glory
And power
Forever
And ever.
To Him be glory
And power
Forever,
Amen. (Together)

1069

TO YOUR MAJESTY,
And Your beauty I surrender.
To Your holiness,
And Your love I surrender.
For You are an awesome God who is mighty,
You deserve my deepest praise;
With all of my heart,
With all of my life I surrender.

1070

VISIT US, O LORD, with Your awesome presence.
Dwell in our midst in Your glory and power,
In Your strength and in Your love.

This is our cry, O Lord,
Let Your presence fill this place,
Fill this place.
(Repeat)

1071 Mick Gisbey.

WAITING FOR YOUR SPIRIT,
Thirsty for Your Spirit;
Touching us, Lord, as we pray,
Filling our lives with You again.
Fall on us, Lord,
As we call on You.

1072 Matt Redman.

WAKE UP, MY SOUL,
Worship the Lord of truth and life.
Have strength, my heart,
Press on as one who seeks the prize.
I'll run for You, my God and King,
I'll run as one who runs to win.
I'm pressing on, not giving in.
I will run, I will run for You, my King.

And Spirit come, give life to us,
Come breathe the Father's love in us.
Won't You fill us once again?
And we will run and run with Him.
We'll run with strength,
With all our might,
We'll fix our eyes on Jesus Christ;
He has conquered death and sin,
And we will run and run and run
With Him.

1073

Nathan Fellingham.

WAKE UP, WAKE UP O SLEEPER,
And rise from the dead.
(Repeat)

We are His people drawn by grace,
Chosen by His glorious name,
Called to give Him all our praise,
Set apart to worship Him.
We must be humble now and pray,
And turn from all our careless ways,
And in our hearts wait for the hour
For Christ to come in awesome power.

We are called to righteousness,
To be like God in holiness;
So let all slander now subside,
And flee from bitterness and rage.
And soon the night will fade away,
And in its place will come the day;
So we must clothe ourselves in light,
The armour that will help us fight.

Revere the name of the Lord,
And He will shine on you;
He will arise with healing
And set you free.

1074

Maggi Dawn.

WASH ME CLEAN in that cool river;
Wash my soul in the pure water.
Wash me clean in that cool river;
Lord, make me new.

1075

Kevin Prosch.

WE ARE HIS PEOPLE,
He gives us music to sing.
There is a sound now,
Like the sound of the Lord when His enemies flee.
But there is a cry in our hearts,
Like when deep calls unto the deep,
For Your breath of deliverance,
To breathe on the music we so desperately need.

But without Your power
All we have are these simple songs.
If You'd step down from heaven,
Then the gates of hell would surely fall.

Shout to the Lord, shout to the Lord,
Shout to the Lord of Hosts.
Shout to the Lord, shout to the Lord,
Shout to the Lord of Hosts.
And it breaks the heavy yoke, breaks the heavy yoke
When you shout, you shout to the Lord.
It breaks the heavy yoke, breaks the heavy yoke,
When you shout, you shout to the Lord.

1076

Tr. Anders Nyberg.

WE ARE MARCHING IN THE LIGHT OF GOD,
We are marching in the light of God.
(Repeat)

We are marching, marching,
We are marching, marching,
We are marching in the light of God.
(Repeat)

Siyahamb' ekukhanyen' kwenkhos',
Siyahamb' ekukhanyen' kwenkhos'.
(Repeat)

Siyahamba, hamba, siyahamba, hamba,
Siyahamb' ekukhanyen' kwenkhos'.
(Repeat)

We are living in the love of God...

We are moving in the power of God...

1077 Lex Loizides.

WE ARE MARCHING TO A DIFFERENT ANTHEM,
We are dancing to a different song;
And our hearts have come alive with freedom,
Mercy has come, the God of mercy has come.
He is moving through the towns and cities,
He is binding up the broken ones;
And His healing hand is working wonders,
See how they come, He sets them free when they come.
And I sing:

I love the God of heaven,
I love His precious Son;
And in the Holy Spirit,
He's making us strong,
And giving us the victory.
I love the God of heaven,
I love His precious Son;
And in the Holy Spirit,
He's making us strong,
And giving us a victory song.

He is training up our hands for battle,
And equipping us to take the land;
For the promises to us are mighty,
We will be strong, and move together as one.

We are heading for our finest hour,
When our Saviour will be magnified,
And His glory will outshine all others:
Jesus is Lord, let Him be praised and adored.
And I sing:

1078

Bob Fitts.

WE ARE SALT and we are the light;
We've come to break the powers of night,
And by the love of God proclaim His liberty.
We're ambassadors of grace,
In His name we take this place;
Lord, let Your will be done,
Let Your kingdom come,
Lord, let it rain, let it rain.

Let Your blessings pour
On the nations, Lord, let it rain.
Let Your blessings pour
On the nations, Lord, let it rain.
As we sing Your praises,
Break the curses, let it rain.
Hear Your people praying,
Send Your blessing, let it rain.
Oh, let it rain.

You have won the fight, O Lord;
By Your death our life's been restored,
And You have risen now
To vanquish all our foes.
Come, abolish every curse
O'er the nations of the earth;
In Your name we'll go,
To proclaim You rose to live and reign.
Lord, come and reign.

1079

Kevin Prosch.

WE ARE THE ARMY OF GOD,
Sons of Abraham,
We are a chosen generation.
Under a covenant,
Washed by His precious blood,
Filled with the mighty Holy Ghost.

And I hear the sound of the coming rain,
As we sing the praise to the great I AM.
And the sick are healed,
And the dead shall rise,
And Your church is the army that was prophesied.

1080

Paul Oakley.

WE ARE YOUR INHERITANCE,
We are Your reward.
(Repeat)
And You're our glory
And the lifter of our heads;
You're our glory
And the lifter of our heads.

Listen, can you hear it?
The Spirit and the Bride.
(Repeat)
Whisper 'Jesus!
Maranatha! Come!'
Whisper 'Jesus!
Maranatha! Come!'

O come, O come to us!
O come, O come to us!
Jesus, Jesus, Jesus!
O come, O come to us!

1081

Richard Lewis.

WE ASK YOU, O LORD,
For the rain of Your Spirit.
We ask You, O Lord,
For the rain of Your Spirit.
For now is the time,
For now is the time
Of the latter rain,
Of the latter rain.

Send Your rain, cleanse us by Your word;
Let us be Your pure and radiant Bride.
Make us strong, prepare us for revival;
Let us see the nations turn their hearts,
Let us see the nations turn their hearts,
Let us see the nations turn their hearts
To You, to You.

Send Your rain, mercy from heaven.
Send Your rain, the grace of Your Son.
Send Your rain, Word of Your power,
Send Your rain, come fill everyone.
(Repeat)

1082

David & Nathan Fellingham.

WE BEHOLD YOUR GLORY,
Fountain of life, the Lord Jesus Christ.
Lord of the universe,
You die in weakness;
Strong Deliverer,
How You were wounded.
Sustainer of life,
Disfigured and shamed,
This is the medicine
That saves and heals us.
A crown of thorns

Was placed on Your brow;
Though You were scourged,
Blow after blow,
By Your stripes we are healed.

We behold Your glory,
Fountain of life, the Lord Jesus Christ.
Though You were fettered,
We are delivered;
Though You were condemned,
We are absolved.
Though You were exposed
To mocking and shame,
We are established
And raised up in honour.
Though You were laid
In the dust of death,
Though You went down
To hell's darkest depths,
The kingdom of heaven is ours.

1083

Ian Smale.

WE BELIEVE IN HEBREWS THIRTEEN, EIGHT,
Jesus Christ is never out of date.
If it's yesterday or today, or forever more,
Jesus stays the same and that is great.

1084

Viola Grafstrom.

WE BOW DOWN and confess
You are Lord in this place.
We bow down and confess
You are Lord in this place.
You are all I need;
It's Your face I seek.
In the presence of Your light
We bow down, we bow down.

1085

Kevin Prosch.

WE CONFESS THE SINS OF OUR NATION,
And, Lord, we are guilty
Of a prayerless life.
We've turned away our hearts from Your laws,
And have taken for granted Your unchanging
grace.
Turn away this curse from our country;
We say that we've robbed You,
And our storehouses are bare.
Open wide the floodgates of heaven,
Rebuke the devourer so we may not be destroyed.

You said that if we'd humble ourselves
And begin to pray,
You would heal our barren land,
And cleanse us with Your rain.

Don't pass us by,
Let this be the generation, Lord,
That lifts up Your name to all the world.
Save us, O God,
Save a people for Yourself, O Lord,
Let the fear of the Lord be a standard.
Save us, O God,
Cleanse us from our unfaithfulness,
Let the place where we live
Be called a house of prayer.

1086

Mark Altrogge.

WE GIVE THANKS TO YOU, O Lord,
Almighty God,
The One who is, who was
And is to come.

You've taken up Your power
And begun to reign,
The nations bow before the Holy One.

Now Your salvation,
And Your power and Your kingdom
Have all come,
And You are Lord of all.
The accuser of the brothers
Has been hurled down forever,
Overcome by the blood,
Overcome by the blood,
Overcome by the blood of the Lamb.

1087

Chris Falson.

WE HAVE A VISION for this nation;
We share a dream for this land.
We join with angels in celebration,
By faith we speak revival to this land.

Where every knee shall bow and worship You,
And every tongue confess that You are Lord;
Give us an open heaven, anoint our prayers this day,
And move Your sovereign hand across this nation.

1088

Stuart Garrard.

WE HAVE CALLED ON YOU, LORD,
And You have heard us.
We have called on Your name,
And You have answered.
Mercy has triumphed over judgement.
Mercy has triumphed over judgement.

You have stretched out Your hand,
And You have touched us,
Sent us Your holy fire,
And You have purged us.
Light has triumphed over darkness.
Light has triumphed over darkness.

We love You, and sing to You,
God of our salvation.
You've rescued us and we declare
Your glory to the nations.
We give our lives, a living sacrifice,
Empty and ready to be filled
With Your power.

1089

Robert Newey.

WE HAVE COME TO SEEK YOUR FACE,
Filled with wonder at Your grace,
Amazed at how You've come
And touched our lives.
But even as we've felt Your touch,
Desire for You has grown so much,
It only serves to make us realise
That the way ahead is in Your strength alone.
So we stand before You now and we cry,
'Lord, lead us on!'

'Cause after all You've brought us through,
We find we're even more dependent on You,
Not in power, not in might,
But through Your Spirit's guiding light.
We're driven by the things He says,
And glory in our weaknesses,
And knowing how we need You now, we come:
Here we stand before You.

And we will wait for You, wait for You;
Show us, Lord, what You would have us do.
We will wait for You, wait for You;
Show us, Lord, what You would have us do.

1090

Martin Smith.

WE HAVE FLOODED THE ALTAR with our tears;
We have wearied You, Lord, with our words.
Great God, our promises we've broken,
O Lord, forgive me.

You are breaking the pride in our hearts;
You have given us tears for the lost.
You crown the humble with salvation;
O Lord, humble me.

So lead me, oh lead me into Your arms;
I will be safe in the shadow of Your wing.
Lead me, oh lead me into Your arms;
I will be safe in Almighty.

You have paid back our sin with Your love;
Lover's arms You have offered us.
Faithful One, raise up a faithful people
Who find their treasure here.

1091

Paul Oakley.

WE HAVE PRAYED THAT YOU WOULD HAVE MERCY;
We believe from heaven You've heard.
Heal our land, so dry and so thirsty;
We have strayed so far from You, Lord.
Your cloud appeared on the horizon,
Small as a man's hand.

But now You're near,
Filling our vision,
Pour out Your Spirit again.

I felt the touch of Your wind on my face:
I feel the first drops of rain.

Let it rain, let it rain.
I will not be the same.
Let it rain, rain on me.
Let it pour down on me,
Let it rain.

Let it rain, let it rain,
Let it rain, let it rain on me.
Let it rain, let it rain,
Let it rain.

1092 Stuart Townend.

WE HAVE SUNG OUR SONGS OF VICTORY,
We have prayed to You for rain;
We have cried for Your compassion
To renew the land again.
Now we're standing in Your presence,
More hungry than before;
Now we're on Your steps of mercy,
And we're knocking at Your door.

How long before You drench the barren land?
How long before we see Your righteous hand?
How long before Your name is lifted high?
How long before the weeping turns to songs of joy?

Lord, we know Your heart is broken
By the evil that You see,
And You've stayed Your hand of judgement
For You plan to set men free.

But the land is still in darkness,
And we've fled from what is right;
We have failed the silent children
Who will never see the light.

But I know a day is coming
When the deaf will hear His voice,
When the blind will see their Saviour,
And the lame will leap for joy.
When the widow finds a Husband
Who will always love His bride,
And the orphan finds a Father
Who will never leave her side.

How long before Your glory lights the skies?
How long before Your radiance lifts our eyes?
How long before Your fragrance fills the air?
How long before the earth resounds with songs of joy?

1093

Noel Richards.

WELCOME, KING OF KINGS!
How great is Your name.
You come in majesty
Forever to reign.

You rule the nations,
They shake at the sound of Your name.
To You is given all power,
And You shall reign.

Let all creation bow down
At the sound of Your name.
Let every tongue now confess,
The Lord God reigns.

1094

David Fellingham.

WE LIFT UP OUR HEADS,
And we will sing our praise
To Him who sits on the throne.
We lift up our heads
To the King of kings,
Who reigns in heaven and earth.

Holy and mighty,
Awesome in power,
Full of compassion
And love.

Glorious in holiness,
Fearful in praises,
Working His wonders
In us.

1095

Martin Smith.

WELL, I HEAR THEY'RE SINGING in the streets
That Jesus is alive,
And all creation shouts aloud
That Jesus is alive.
Now surely we can all be changed
'cause Jesus is alive;
And everybody here can know
That Jesus is alive.

And I will live for all my days
To raise a banner of truth and light,
To sing about my Saviour's love—
And the best thing that happened,
It was the day I met You.

I've found Jesus.
I've found Jesus.
I've found Jesus.
I've found Jesus.

Well, I feel like dancing in the streets
'Cause Jesus is alive,
To join with all who celebrate
That Jesus is alive.
The joy of God is in this town
'Cause Jesus is alive;
For everybody's seen the truth
That Jesus is alive.

And I will live for all my days...

Well, You lifted me from where I was,
Set my feet upon a rock,
Humbled that You even know about me.
Now I have chosen to believe,
Believing that You've chosen me;
I was lost but now I've found...

1096

Bob Baker.

WELL, I THANK YOU, LORD,
That You are my Saviour;
You're my strength
And You're the Rock on which I stand.
You give me life,
And a grace that's greater,
When I humble myself
Beneath Your mighty hand.

You bring times of refreshing,
You bring times of refreshing,
You bring times of refreshing to my soul.

When I'm weary from the fight,
And trying to do what's right,
You bring times of refreshing to my soul.

For the day will come
When we'll all be gathered,
And the sun will rise with healing in its wings;
And all the years of pain
Won't seem to matter,
When our eyes behold
Our Teacher and our King.

1097 Chris Bowater.

WE'RE HERE FOR THE HARVEST,
Get ready to reap,
The call is for action,
It's not time to sleep.
We're here for the harvest,
The yield will be great;
The fields are now ripened,
So don't hesitate.

There's need for more labourers,
For many, not few,
The challenge set before us
Is who? And we cry:
Lord of the harvest,
In this day of Your power,
Hear the anthem of voices: 'send me!'

Send me, send me,
Lord of the harvest, send me!
Send me, send me,
Lord of the harvest, send me!

The Spirit is upon us,
To cause the blind to see;
The Spirit of the Sovereign Lord
To set the captive free.
The homeless and the needy
Can no longer be ignored,
And all oppressed will celebrate
The favour of the Lord.

There's need for more labourers...

1098

Carol Owen.

WE REJOICE IN THE GOODNESS OF OUR GOD,
We rejoice in the wonders of Your favour.
You've set the captives free,
You've caused the blind to see,
Hallelujah,
You give us liberty, hallelujah.

Always the same, You never change,
And Your mercies are new every day.
Compassionate and gracious,
Our faithful loving God,
Slow to anger, rich in love.

You give us hope, You give us joy,
You give us fulness of life to enjoy.
Our Shepherd and Provider,
Our God who's always there,
Never failing, always true.

1099

Matt Redman.

WE'RE LOOKING TO YOUR PROMISE of old,
That if we pray and humble ourselves,
You will come and heal our land,
You will come,
You will come.

We're looking to the promise You made,
That if we turn and look to Your face,
You will come and heal our land,
You will come,
You will come to us.

Lord, send revival, start with me.
For I am one of unclean lips,
And my eyes have seen the King;
Your glory I have glimpsed.
Send revival, start with me.

1100

Ian White.

WE'RE REACHING OUT TO YOU AGAIN.
We're in the upper room again.
We feel the Spirit's wave,
We're in pre-revival days.
We're kneeling on the floor again.
We're crying out for more again.
We're seeking for Your face
We're in pre-revival days.

You say where our treasure is,
There is our heart.
You say where our treasure is,
There is our heart.

We're looking at our lives again.
Your love has filled our eyes again.
We cherish Your embrace,
We're in pre-revival days.
We're praying for the lost again.
The hardened heart is soft again.
No one is turned away,
We're in pre-revival days.

We're talking in the streets again.
You're showing us what to speak again.
The demons scream with rage,
We're in pre-revival days.

But a single song
Can never change our ways,
So we cry to You, Lord,
You are mighty to save.

Jesus out in front again.
Jesus on our tongues again.
We're rising up in faith
To see revival days.
We're praying for our land again.
You've stayed Your patient hand again.
This nation needs Your grace
To see revival days.

1101

Richard Lewis & Chris Cartwright.

WE'RE SO THANKFUL TO YOU,
We're so grateful for the things You've done,
That You died for us on the cross—
Such a painful death,
That You paid the price for us,
You paid the price for us.

And we say thank You, Lord.
We say thank You, Lord.
We say thank You for what You have done.
And we say thank You, Lord.
We say thank You, Lord.
We say thank You
For the things You have done.

It's so wonderful that you rose,
Victorious over death and hell.
All authority is now Yours,
And the Comforter
You have sent in fulness to us,
You have come to us.

1102

Stuart Garrard.

WE'RE STANDING HERE with open hearts,
Our voices joined in unity.
We know we don't lead perfect lives,
And we cry to You for mercy.
Father in heaven, we honour Your name,
That we might bring You glory and fame;
Pour out Your Spirit upon us we pray,
To heal and deliver and save.

This is our heart cry;
This is our heart cry.
(Repeat)

We stand before the throne of grace,
A people for Your possession;
We hunger and thirst, we seek Your face,
Come touch us with Your presence.
Father in heaven, holy and true,
Stretch out Your hand, let power break through;
Pour out Your Spirit upon us today,
To heal and deliver and save.

1103

Lex Loizides.

WE STAND TOGETHER before our Saviour,
We stand together in the cause of our God.
We have a vision, we've been commissioned
To raise a banner in the name of our God.

Once, when we were dead in our sin,
Our hearts were turned away,
But then the light of Christ broke in
And made us live again.
And if You could heal our blindness,
You can save our nation too,
So we give ourselves this day to follow You.

We'll preach the gospel, we'll tell the people.
About a Saviour who has died on a cross.
With true compassion, without distraction,
While we have time we will deliver the lost.

Someday soon the King will come
With glory, power and might,
And all the hosts of heaven and hell
Will bow before the light.
And the nations will be gathered
For the righteous Judge will come,
And the blood-bought church
Will join the Risen One.

1104

Sue Rinaldi.

WE WANNA CHANGE THIS WORLD,
We wanna change this world.
(Repeat)

So wave those flags of justice
Over the nations,
And hit those drums of peace
Among the peoples.
We hear the sound of history in the making,
Let God's love run around the earth
And bring freedom!

So hold each other's hands
Across the oceans,
And play those chords of peace
Among the peoples.
We hear the sound of reconciliation:
Let God's love dance around the earth
And bring freedom!

And we wanna change this world
As we live out holy lives.
And we wanna change this world
As You wash our motives clean.
(Repeat)
Oh, wash us clean!

1105

Doug Horley.

WE WANT TO SEE JESUS LIFTED HIGH,
A banner that flies across this land,
That all men might see the truth and know
He is the way to heaven.
(Repeat)

We want to see, We want to see,
We want to see Jesus lifted high.
We want to see, we want to see,
We want to see Jesus lifted high.

Step by step we're moving forward,
Little by little taking ground,
Every prayer a powerful weapon,
Strongholds come tumbling down,
And down, and down, and down.

We're gonna see, we're gonna see,
We're gonna see Jesus lifted high.
We're gonna see, we're gonna see,
We're gonna see Jesus lifted high.

1106

Steve Cantellow & Matt Redman.

WE WILL GIVE OURSELVES NO REST
Till Your kingdom comes on earth;
You've positioned watchmen on the walls.
Now our prayers will flow like tears,
For You've shared Your heart with us;
God of heaven, on our knees we fall.
Come down in power,
Reveal Your heart again;
Come hear our cries,
The tears that plead for rain.

We're knocking,
Knocking on the door of heaven,
We're crying,
Crying for this generation;
We're praying for Your name to be known
In all of the earth.
We're watching,
Watching on the walls to see You,
We're looking,
Looking for a time of breakthrough;
We're praying for Your word to bear fruit
In all of the earth, in all of the earth.

1107

Dave Bilbrough.

WE WILL TEAR DOWN EVERY STRONGHOLD
Through the power of His word.
We will seek to bring His kingdom in,
Make a way for His return.

We will tell of His salvation,
For the church of Christ is called
To bring healing to the nations,
See His righteousness restored.

Satan is defeated,
Christ has overcome,
Seated at the Father's hand,
Lord, on earth may Your will now be done.

1108

Dennis Jernigan.

WE WILL WORSHIP THE LAMB OF GLORY,
We will worship the King of kings;
We will worship the Lamb of Glory,
We will worship the King.

And with our hands lifted high
We will worship and sing,
And with our hands lifted high
We come before You rejoicing.
With our hands lifted high to the sky,
When the world wonders why,
We'll just tell them we're loving our King.
Oh, we'll just tell them we're loving our King.
Yes, we'll just tell them loving our King.

Bless the name of the Lamb of Glory,
I bless the name of the King of kings;
Bless the name of the Lamb of Glory,
Bless the name of the King.

1109

Martin Smith.

WHAT A FRIEND I'VE FOUND,
Closer than a brother;
I have felt Your touch,
More intimate than lovers.

Jesus, Jesus,
Jesus, Friend forever.
(Repeat)

What a hope I've found,
More faithful than a mother;
It would break my heart
To ever lose each other.

1110 Geoff Bullock.

WHATEVER I HAVE GAINED,
Whatever I have done,
I leave it all behind to follow You.
The things that I attained,
The goals I may have gained,
A prize or any glory of my own.

For I am lost without Your love,
All things are loss without Your love;
For I am lost without Your love,
All things are loss without Your love.

The wonder of Your love,
The wonder of Your grace;
To gain You and to know You as my Lord.
That I am found in You,
Your righteousness alone,
Is more than I could dream or ever ask.

1111 Bryn & Sally Haworth.

WHAT KIND OF LOVE IS THIS
That gave itself for me?
I am the guilty one,
Yet I go free.

What kind of love is this,
A love I've never known;
I didn't even know His name—
What kind of love is this?

What kind of man is this,
That died in agony?
He who had done no wrong
Was crucified for me.
What kind of man is this,
Who laid aside His throne
That I may know the love of God—
What kind of man is this?

By grace I have been saved;
It is the gift of God.
He destined me to be His son,
Such is His love.
No eye has ever seen,
No ear has ever heard,
Nor has the heart of man conceived
What kind of love is this.

1112

Matt Redman.

WHEN CAN I GO AND MEET WITH GOD?
My soul is weak, my body tired.
Can it be here, can it be now?
I need to find that place again.

When can I come and meet You, God?
I thirst inside for heaven's touch.
Let it be here, let it be now;
I need to find that place again...

Where deep calls to deep
In the roar of Your waterfalls,
You're calling me
With the force of Your love.

Let Your waves sweep
Over all the dry places, Lord;
Usher me in to the depths of Your heart,
Where deep calls to deep,
Where deep calls to deep,
Where deep calls to deep,
Where deep calls to deep.

I want to know Your risen power.
I need to share Your sufferings;
And as I die to my own will,
Lord, raise me to that place again.

1113

Matt Redman.

WHEN THE MUSIC FADES, all is stripped away,
And I simply come;
Longing just to bring something that's of worth
That will bless Your heart.

I'll bring You more than a song,
For a song in itself
Is not what You have required.
You search much deeper within
Through the way things appear;
You're looking into my heart.

I'm coming back to the heart of worship,
And it's all about You,
All about You, Jesus.
I'm sorry, Lord, for the thing I've made it,
When it's all about You,
All about You, Jesus.

King of endless worth, no one could express
How much You deserve.
Though I'm weak and poor, all I have is Yours,
Every single breath.

1114 Noel Richards.

WHEN WE'RE IN TROUBLE,
When there are cares;
When faith is shaken up,
When we despair,
We call on Jesus,
Give Him our thanks;
We let His peace and joy
Come to our hearts.

We're gonna keep on praying,
Keep on praying.
We're gonna keep on praying,
Keep on praying.

When there is sickness,
When there is pain,
There is a healing touch,
Each time we pray.
God always listens,
Cares for our needs;
Prayers of the righteous one
Have power indeed.

Prayers for the nation,
Prayers for the world.
Prayers for the government,
Prayers for the church.
Prayers for the seekers,
Prayers for the saints,
Praying that people will come to faith.

1115

Kevin Prosch.

WHEN YOU'VE BEEN BROKEN, broken to pieces,
And your heart begins to faint,
'Cause you don't understand.
And when there is nothing
To rake from the ashes,
And you can't even walk
Onto the fields of praise.
But I bow down and kiss the Son.
Oh, I bow down and kiss the Son.

When the rock falls, falls upon you,
And you get ground to dust,
No music for your pain.
You open the windows,
The windows of heaven,
And then You opened me,
And You crushed me like a rose.
But I bow down and kiss the Son.
Oh, I bow down and kiss the Son.
Oh, I bow down and kiss the Son.

Let the praise of the Lord be in my mouth,
Let the praise of the Lord be in my mouth.

Though You slay me, I will trust You, Lord.
(Repeat x4)

1116

Tommy Walker.

WHERE THERE ONCE WAS ONLY HURT,
He gave His healing hand;
Where there once was only pain,
He brought comfort like a friend.

I feel the sweetness of His love
Piercing my darkness.
I see the bright and morning sun
As it ushers in His joyful gladness.

He's turned my mourning into dancing again,
He's lifted my sorrow.
I can't stay silent, I must sing
For His joy has come.

His anger lasts for a moment in time;
But His favour is here
And will be on me for all my lifetime.

1117

Paul Oakley.

WHO IS THERE LIKE YOU,
And who else would give their life for me,
Even suffering in my place?
And who could repay You?
All of creation looks to You,
And You provide for all You have made.

So I'm lifting up my hands,
Lifting up my voice,
Lifting up Your name,
And in Your grace I rest,
For Your love has come to me
And set me free.
And I'm trusting in Your word,
Trusting in Your cross,
Trusting in Your blood
And all Your faithfulness,
For Your power at work in me
Is changing me.

1118

Stuart Townend.

WHO PAINTS THE SKIES into glorious day?
Only the splendour of Jesus.
Who breathes His life into fists of clay?
Only the splendour of Jesus.
Who shapes the valleys and brings the rain?
Only the splendour of Jesus.
Who makes the desert to live again?
Only the splendour of Jesus.

Teach every nation His marvellous ways;
Each generation shall sing His praise.

He is wonderful, He is glorious,
Clothed in righteousness,
Full of tenderness.
Come and worship Him,
He's the Prince of life,
He will cleanse our hearts
In His river of fire.

Who hears the cry of the barren one?
Only the mercy of Jesus.
Who breaks the curse of the heart of stone?
Only the mercy of Jesus.
Who storms the prison and sets men free,
Only the mercy of Jesus.
Purchasing souls for eternity?
Only the mercy of Jesus.

1119

Alex Muir.

WHOSE LIPS WILL PLEAD
For the people of this land?
Who'll stand in the gap,
And who'll build up the wall,

Before the long day of God's patience is over,
Before the night comes
When His judgement will fall?

And whose eyes will weep
For the people of this land?
And whose hearts will break
For the hearts made of stone,
For those who are walking out into darkness,
Away from God's love,
Without Christ, so alone?

And whose ears can hear
What the Spirit is saying
To those who are willing
To watch and to pray?
Pray on till God's light
Fills the skies over this land,
The light of revival that brings a new day.

1120

Graham Maule & John L. Bell.

WILL YOU COME AND FOLLOW ME
If I but call your name?
Will you go where you don't know
And never be the same?
Will you let My love be shown,
Will you let My name be known,
Will you let My life be grown in you,
And you in Me?

Will you leave yourself behind
If I but call your name?
Will you care for cruel and kind
And never be the same?
Will you risk the hostile stare,
Should your life attract or scare?
Will you let Me answer prayer
In you and you in Me?

Will you let the blinded see
If I but call your name?
Will you set the prisoners free
And never be the same?
Will you kiss the leper clean,
And do such as this unseen,
And admit to what I mean
In you and you in Me?

Will you love the 'you' you hide
If I but call your name?
Will you quell the fear inside
And never be the same?
Will you use the faith you've found
To reshape the world around,
Through My sight and touch and sound
In you and you in Me?

Lord, Your summons echoes true
When You but call my name.
Let me turn and follow You
And never be the same.
In Your company I'll go
Where Your love and footsteps show;
Thus I'll move and live and grow
In You and You in me.

1121

Ruth Dryden.

WITHIN THE VEIL I now would come,
Into the holy place, to look upon Thy face.
I see such beauty there, no other can compare;
I worship Thee, my Lord, within the veil.

1122 Carol Owen.

WORTHY IS THE LAMB,
Worthy is the Lamb,
Worthy is the Lamb who was slain.
(Repeat)

My Lord and Saviour,
My great Redeemer,
Your blood has purchased me for God.
My Lord and Saviour,
My great Redeemer,
You came to set the captives free.

Holy is the Lamb . . .

Jesus, You're the Lamb . . .

Glory to the Lamb . . .

1123 Carl Tuttle.

YET THIS WILL I CALL TO MIND,
And therefore I will hope,
Because of the Lord's great love
I've been redeemed.
The Lord is gracious and kind
To all who call on His name,
Because of the Lord's great love
I've been redeemed.

Because of the Lord's great love,
Because of the Lord's great love,
Because of the Lord's great love
I've been redeemed.

I know of His steadfast love,
His mercy renewed each day,
Because of the Lord's great love
I've been redeemed.
Washed in the blood of the Lamb,
Guiltless for ever I stand,
Because of the Lord's great love
I've been redeemed.

1124

Ian White.

YOU ARE MERCIFUL TO ME,
You are merciful to me,
You are merciful to me, my Lord.
(Repeat)

Every day my disobedience
Grieves Your loving heart;
But then redeeming love breaks through,
And causes me to worship You.

(Men – Women echo))
Redeemer,
Saviour,
Healer
And Friend.
Every day
Renew my ways,
Fill me with love
That never ends.

1125 Craig Musseau.

YOU ARE MIGHTY,
You are holy,
You are awesome in Your power.
You have risen, You have conquered,
You have beaten the power of death.

Hallelujah, we will rejoice.
Hallelujah, we will rejoice.

1126 Brian Doerksen.

YOU ARE MY KING, (You are my King)
And I love You.
You are my King, (You are my King)
And I worship You.

Kneeling before You now,
All of my life I gladly give to You.
Placing my hopes and dreams
In Your hands,
I give my heart to You.

I love You, love You, Jesus.
Yes, I love You, love You, Jesus,
My King.

1127 Noel & Tricia Richards.

YOU ARE MY PASSION,
Love of my life,
Friend and companion, my Lover.
All of my being
Longs for Your touch;
With all my heart I love You.

Now You will draw me close to You,
Gather me in Your arms;
Let me hear the beating of Your heart,
O my Jesus,
O my Jesus.

1128

Wynne Goss.

YOU ARE RIGHTEOUS in all Your ways,
You are good, You are good.
You are truthful in all You say,
You are good, You are good.

And I bow my knee before You,
In honour of Your name,
For You alone are worthy,
Worthy of my praise,
Worthy of my praise.

You are holy, faithful and true,
You are good, You are good.
You are gracious in all You do,
You are good, You are good.

1129

Tommy Walker.

YOU ARE THE GREAT I AM,
Forever You will be.
Let every angel sing
Of Your perfect authority.
Every knee will bow
And every tongue confess;
You are the great I AM,
The First and Last

Mighty, (Mighty)
Eternal, (Eternal)
Immortal, (Immortal)
Awesome One. (Awesome One)
Mysterious, (Mysterious)
The Wonderful, (the Wonderful)
The Holy One, (the Holy One)
The Beginning and the End.

1130

Steve & Vikki Cook.

YOU ARE THE PERFECT AND RIGHTEOUS GOD
Whose presence bears no sin;
You bid me come to Your holy place:
How can I enter in
When Your presence bears no sin?
Through Him who poured out His life for me,
The atoning Lamb of God,
Through Him and His work alone I boldly come.

I come by the blood, I come by the cross,
Where Your mercy flows
From hands pierced for me.
For I dare not stand on my righteousness,
My every hope rests on what Christ has done,
And I come by the blood.

You are the high and exalted King,
The One the angels fear;
So far above me in every way,
Lord, how can I draw near
To the One the angels fear?
Through Him who laid down His life for me
And ascended to Your side,
Through Him, through Jesus alone I boldly come.

1131

Per Soetorp.

YOU ARE WONDERFUL,
Counsellor, Mighty God.
You are Prince of Peace,
Our Father forever more.
You're the Alpha and Omega,
Lord of all lords.
You are Wonderful,
Counsellor, Mighty God.

1132

John Pantry.

YOU ARE WORTHY TO RECEIVE
All the honour and praise.
Lamb of God, Prince of Peace,
We lift high Your name.

For Yours is the greatness,
The power and the glory;
Lord of the nations,
Have mercy on us.
Though heaven be shaken,
And earth's kingdoms fall,
We will still worship You.

In the footsteps of our King,
We walk unafraid;
Though the battle may rage,
Our praises will ring.

1133

Terry Butler.

YOU BLESS MY LIFE, and heal me inside,
Over and over again.
You touched my heart and brought peace of mind,
Over and over again.

All I can say is I love You.
All I can say is I need You.
All I can say is I thank You, Lord,
For all that You've done in my life.

You've been so kind and patient with me,
Over and over again.
When I have strayed You showed me the way,
Over and over again.

1134

Robert Newey.

YOU CAME to heal the brokenhearted;
You came to make the blind eyes see.
Your light is burning now within us,
As Your word of truth sets us free.

And we will fill the earth with the love of God
That's been shed abroad in our hearts,
Share with every nation and every land
The grace that He imparts.
And we will sing a new song of joy and peace,
A resounding trumpet call,
Causing hearts to rise, opening eyes to see
That Jesus, Jesus is Lord of all.

You come in all Your mighty power,
You come to bring the latter rain;
We know You've filled us with Your Spirit
And a love we cannot contain.

You'll come in glory and splendour,
You'll come to reign upon the earth;
We know we'll live with You forever
And declare Your mighty worth.

1135

Mark Altrogge.

YOU HAVE BECOME FOR US WISDOM;
You have become for us righteousness.
You have become our salvation;
You have become all our holiness.

All that we need is found in You;
Oh, all that we need is in You.
All that we need is found in You;
You are our all in all.
You have become our all in all.

You have become our provision;
In union with You we have victory.
In You we have died and have risen;
You are our great hope of glory.

1136

Andy Park.

YOU HAVE CALLED US CHOSEN,
A royal priesthood,
A holy nation,
We belong to You.
(Repeat)

Take our lives as a sacrifice;
Shine in us Your holy light.
Purify our hearts' desire;
Be to us a consuming fire.

You have shown us mercy,
You have redeemed us;
Our hearts cry 'Father,
We belong to You.'
(Repeat)

1137

Alun Leppitt.

YOU HAVE LIFTED UP THE HUMBLE,
Filled the hungry with good things;
Shown Your mercy to the fearful,
You have healing in Your wings.
The rich will leave with nothing,
But the poor will have it all,
And the pure in heart will see their holy God.

You will light the road from darkness,
As You lead us to Your throne;
You give strength to the weary,
And shelter from the storm.
You pour out living waters
So we will never thirst,
And You wipe away the tears from our eyes.

Holy is Your name,
Holy is Your name;
Perfect grace and rich in love,
Your mercy never ends.
Holy is Your name,
Holy is Your name;
Precious Lamb of sacrifice,
Forever You will reign.

You bring justice to the nations,
Salvation's at Your hand;
With your blood You made the purchase
From every tribe and land,

To be priests within Your kingdom,
Your Spirit's on us all
To show the love and favour of the Lord.

1138 Tom Davis & Kevin Prosch.

YOU HAVE TAKEN THE PRECIOUS
From the worthless and given us
Beauty for ashes, love for hate.
You have chosen the weak things
Of the world to shame that which is strong,
And the foolish things to shame the wise.

You are help to the helpless,
Strength to the stranger,
And a father to the child that's left alone.
And the thirsty You've invited
To come to the waters,
And those who have no money, come and buy.

So come, so come.
So come, so come.

Behold the days are coming
For the Lord has promised,
That the ploughman will overtake the reaper.
And our hearts will be the threshing floor,
And the move of God we've cried out for
Will come, it will surely come.

For You will shake the heavens,
And fill Your house with glory,
And turn the shame of the outcast into praise.
And all creation groans and waits
For the Spirit and the Bride to say
The word that Your heart has longed to hear.

1139

YOU MAKE YOUR FACE TO SHINE ON ME,
And that my soul knows very well;
You lift me up, I'm cleansed and free,
And that my soul knows very well.

When mountains fall I'll stand
By the power of Your hand,
And in Your heart of hearts I'll dwell,
And that my soul knows very well.
(Repeat)

Joy and strength each day I'll find,
And that my soul knows very well;
Forgiveness, hope I know is mine,
And that my soul knows very well.

1140

YOU NEVER PUT A LIGHT UNDER A DIRTY OLD BUCKET.
You never put a light under a dirty old bucket.
You never put a light under a dirty old bucket
If you want light to shine around, round, round.

Shine, shine around, round round.
Shine, shine around, round, round.
Shine a light that everyone can see.
Lord, help me let my little light shine,
Not just Sundays, all the time,
So friends give praise to You
When they see me.

1141

Carol Mundy.

YOU'RE AMAZING,
An amazing mighty God,
Full of compassion and true.
You're a loving heavenly Father
To whom all praise is due.
You're so amazing,
Father, I love You.

1142

Geoff Bullock.

YOU RESCUED ME, and picked me up,
A living hope of grace revealed,
A life transformed in righteousness,
O Lord You have rescued me.
Forgiving me, You healed my heart,
And set me free from sin and death.
You brought me life, You made me whole,
O Lord, You have rescued me.

And You loved me before I knew You,
And You knew me for all time.
I've been created in Your image,
O Lord.
And You bought me, and You sought me,
Your blood poured out for me;
A new creation in Your image,
O Lord.
You rescued me, You rescued me.

1143

Robin Mark.

YOU'RE THE LION OF JUDAH,
The Lamb that was slain,
You ascended to heaven
And ever more will reign;

At the end of the age
When the earth You reclaim,
You will gather the nations before You.
And the eyes of all men will be
Fixed on the Lamb who was crucified,
For with wisdom and mercy and justice
You'll reign at Your Father's side.

And the angels will cry:
'Hail the Lamb
Who was slain for the world,
Rule in power.'
And the earth will reply:
'You shall reign
As the King of all kings
And the Lord of all lords.'

There's a shield in our hand
And a sword at our side,
There's a fire in our spirit
That cannot be denied;
As the Father has told us,
For these You have died,
For the nations that gather before You.
And the ears of all men need to hear
Of the Lamb who was crucified,
Who descended to hell yet was raised up
To reign at the Father's side.

1144

Darlene Zschech.

YOUR EYE IS ON THE SPARROW,
And Your hand, it comforts me.
From the ends of the earth
To the depths of my heart,
Let Your mercy and strength be seen.

You call me to Your purpose,
As angels understand.
For Your glory may You draw all men,
As Your love and grace demands.

And I will run to You,
To Your words of truth;
Not by might, not by power
But by the Spirit of God.
Yes, I will run the race,
Till I see Your face.
Oh, let me live in the glory of Your grace.

1145

Chris Falson.

YOUR LOVE LOOKS AFTER ME,
It never fails.
Your word takes care of me,
And keeps my mind on You.
(Repeat)

You are majestic
Through all the earth;
I am Your servant
For the rest of my days.

You are magnificent,
The God of glory;
I'm going to worship You
For the rest of my days,
For the rest of my days,
For the rest of my days.

1146

Peggy Caswell.

YOUR LOVE, O LORD,
It reaches to the heavens;
Your faithfulness,
It reaches to the skies.
Your righteousness is like
The mighty mountains;
How priceless is Your faithful love.

I will exalt You, O Lord,
I will exalt You, O Lord.
Praise Your holy name,
That my heart may sing to You;
I will exalt You, O Lord.

Your name, O Lord,
It is a mighty tower;
Your glory
It covers all the earth.
In Your hands alone
Are strength and power,
All praise be to Your glorious name.

1147

David Wellington.

YOUR NAME IS PEACE
Saviour so holy;
King of righteousness
Merciful and mighty.
God with us,
Revealed to us,
Awesome and eternal God,
Your name is peace.
Wonderful Counsellor,
Everlasting Father,
Lord, Your name is peace,
Your name is peace.

1148

Paul Oakley.

YOUR VOICE IS LIKE THUNDER,
Your eyes like fire;
Your throne is forever,
In unapproachable light.
Your grace is so tender,
Your love like wine;
To You I surrender,
I lay down my life.

And all I want to do . . .

Is to build a house of gold,
Purest silver and costly stones;
Let it stand when the fire comes,
When the day brings Your light.
Be my wisdom and be my strength,
Fill me up with Your faithfulness;
Keep me loving until the end.
Let the fire in Your eyes
See a living sacrifice,
Pleasing in Your sight.

Let me build a house of gold . . .

1149

Dougie Brown.

YOUR WILL, NOT MINE, that is what I desire to see,
Walking in righteousness, and holy liberty.
Your life, not mine, that is what I desire to live,
Forgiving others, as always You forgive.

I bow before Your majesty,
I fall before Your throne;
I cannot understand Your love,
But I claim it as my own.

I rise and stand before You
As a living sacrifice;
I seek to do Your will, O God,
For the rest of my life.

Your voice, not mine, that is what I desire to hear;
Speak in the stillness and whisper in my ear.
Your mind, not mine, that is what I desire to have;
To prophesy Your word, release the captive heart.

Your race, not mine, that is what I desire to run;
To finish off the work that others have begun.
Your work, not mine, that is what I desire to do;
To serve Your purposes, and worship only You.

1150 Dave Dickerson.

YOU SHALL BE HOLY
And in everything be true,
For I, the Lord, am holy,
And My word belongs to you.

Stay in my presence,
Grow strong in My love,
With all the gifts I give you
From My kingdom here above.

We are Your children,
Abba Father, mighty God,
And growing in Your likeness,
Through grace of Jesus' blood.

Inspired by Your Spirit,
Our eternal source of power,
Release us to worship,
And to praise You every hour.

Copyright Addresses

Ateliers et Presses de Taizé, F-71250 Taizé Communauté, Cluny, France.

Karen Barrie, 511 Maple, Wilmette, Illinois 60091, USA.

Kay Chance, Glaubenszentrum 3353 Bad Gandersheim, Germany.

Christian Fellowship of Columbia, 4600 Christian Fellowship Road, Columbia, Missouri 65203, USA.

Church of England Central Board of Finance, Church House, Great Smith Street, London, SW1P 3NZ.

CopyCare, P.O. Box 77, Hailsham, East Sussex, BN27 3EF, UK.

David Higham Associates, 5-8 Lower John Street, Golden Square, London, W1R 3PE, UK.

Daybreak Music Ltd, Silverdale Road, Eastbourne, East Sussex, BN20 7AB, UK.

Timothy Dudley-Smith, 9 Ashlands, Ford, Salisbury, Wiltshire, SP4 6DY, UK.

Gabriel Music, P.O. Box 840999, Houston, Texas 77284-0999, USA.

Grace! Music, 11610 Grandview Road, Kansas City, Missouri 64137, USA.

Heart of David Music, *contact* Grace! Music.

Hi-Fye Music, 8-9 Frith Street, London, W1V 5TZ, UK.

IMP, Southend Road, Woodford Green, Essex, IG8 8HN, UK.

The Independent Music Group, Independent House, 54 Larkshall Road, Chingford, London, E4 6PD, UK.

Josef Weinberger Ltd, 12-14 Mortimer Street, London, W1N 7RD, UK.

Jubilate Hymns, 4 Thorne Park Road, Chelston, Torquay, Devon, TQ2 6RX

Kingdom Faith, Foundry Lane, Horsham, West Sussex, RH13 5PX, UK.

Kingsway's Thankyou Music, P.O. Box 75, Eastbourne, East Sussex, BN23 6NW, UK.

Melva Lea, P.O. Box 2744, Del Mar, California 92014, USA.

Mike and Claire McIntosh, Grace Church, PO Box 24000, Federal Way, Washington 98093, USA.

Len Magee Music, 71 Merridown Drive, Carrara, Queensland 4211, Australia.

Leosong Copyright, *contact* The Independent Music Group.

Make Way Music, P.O. Box 263, Croydon, Surrey, CR9 5AP, UK.

OCP Publications, 5536 N.E. Hassalo, Portland, Oregan 97213, USA.

Oxford University Press, 70 Baker Street, London, W1M 1DJ, UK.

C. Simmonds, 22 St Michael's Road, Bedford, Bedfordshire, MK40 2LT, UK.

Mary Smail, c/o Rev. Tom Smail, 366 Alexandra Road, Croydon, Surrey, CR0 6EU, UK.

Songs for Today, *contact* Windswept Pacific.

Sovereign Music UK, P.O. Box 356, Leighton Buzzard, Bedfordshire, LU7 8WP, UK.

Linda Stassen, New Songs Ministries, R.R. 1 Box 454, Erin, Tennessee 37061, USA.

Warner Chappell Music, *contact* IMP

Wild Goose Resource Group, Iona Community, Pearce Institute, 840 Govan Road, Glasgow, G51 3UU, Scotland, UK.

William Elkin Music Services, Station Road Industrial Estate, Salhouse, Norwich, Norfolk, NR13 6NY, UK.

Windswept Pacific, 27 Queensdale Place, London, W11 4SQ, UK.

Index of Titles and First Lines

This index combines all the songs from the two Large Print editions, with songs from this edition highlighted in **bold**. Please note that author's titles, where different from first line, are shown in *italics*.

Keep in touch!

Kingsway's *Worship Together* is a great way of keeping up to date with new songs and other worship resources. If you would like to find out more about this range of services for you and your church, just fill in your details on the form below, cut it out and send it to us at : Kingsway Music, Lottbridge Drove, Eastbourne, East Sussex, BN23 6NT, UK. Alternatively, you can contact us by telephone on 01323 437708, fax 01323 411970, or e-mail music@kingsway.co.uk, and ask our staff to make sure you are kept informed.

- ☐ Please send me details of how to legally photocopy sheet music.
- ☐ Please send me details of other Kingsway recordings and songbooks.
- ☐ Please send me details of your worship magazine, *Worship Together.*
- ☐ Please send me details of the *Worship Together* Resource pack.
- ☐ Please send me details of the *Worship Together* Seminar programme.

Name (Rev, Mr, Mrs, Miss) --

Address --

Postcode --

Telephone no. --

Church affiliation (eg. House Church, Anglican, etc.)

DATA PROTECTION ACT

If you do not wish to receive information from other Christian organisations or charities please tick. ☐